OUT OF PALMYRA

A CONVERT LOOKS AT THE
PROPHETIC CALLING OF
JOSEPH SMITH

GEORGE W. GIVENS

Parley Street Publishers
Lynchburg, Virginia

Givens, George W., 1932 –
    Out of Palmyra: A Convert Looks at the Prophetic Calling Of Joseph Smith
    Includes bibliographical references.
    1. Mormons – Religion – 19th Century.   2. Joseph Smith

Printed in the United States of America
10 9 8 7 6 5 4 3 2 1

To my mother
who entered the waters
of baptism In her 80th year

"AND NATHANAEL SAID UNTO HIM, CAN THERE ANY GOOD THING COME OUT OF NAZARETH? PHILIP SAITH UNTO HIM COME AND SEE."

JOHN 1:46

"SURELY 'FACTS ARE STUBBORN THINGS'. IT WILL BE AS IT EVER HAD BEEN, THE WORLD WILL PROVE JOSEPH SMITH A TRUE PROPHET BY CIRCUMSTANTIAL EVIDENCE, IN EXPERIMENTS, AS THEY DID MOSES AND ELIJAH."

JOSEPH SMITH

i

TABLE OF CONTENTS

ii

PREFACE

The most basic question skeptics pose when discussing Mormonism is "Why wasn't conclusive evidence of the Book of Mormon provided to convince people like me?" This question is comparable to "Why isn't evidence of God so manifest that there would be no unbelievers?"

The answer to the latter, of course, is rather self-evident to most Christians. It was essential that man and woman be endowed with free agency in order for them to believe or disbelieve, to accept or reject. If God wished for an eternal satisfying relationship with His children, it was necessary that they would willingly return His love and willingly obey His commandments. Compulsion through delineated knowledge of the consequences of rejection could not be a factor in a truly gratifying relationship.

By the same logic, if the evidence of Joseph Smith's prophetic calling were so obviously manifested that no prayer or study was necessary in recognizing it, not only would the concept of religious faith be transgressed, but this additional and persuasive evidence for the redeeming mission of Christ would be so universally apparent that religious faith, the cornerstone of Christianity, could receive a lethal blow. With the necessity for faith in Christ negated by such additional proof of His divine mission, free agency would be lessened in direct proportion to the extent of Gospel obedience resulting from a temporal knowledge of the consequences of obedience or disobedience.

It is not necessary to accept Latter-day Saint theology to understand the importance of free agency and to understand that anything that lessens this God-given attribute lessens the unprejudiced reverence we feel for our Savior. Our greatest hope for eternal life lies not in the conspicuous evidence of Christ's divinity or the patently undisguised veracity of the scriptures, but in a theology that requires sincere prayer and faith in acquiring spiritual knowledge.

The Lord could just as easily have made the mission of the Prophet Joseph evident to the least informed and most skeptical, but doing so would require a redefinition of faith recorded in the Scriptures as "the evidence of things not seen." Why do skeptics, especially those of other faiths, grant other Christians and themselves the privilege of employing faith as a keystone of their theology but deny it to Latter-day Saints? It is certainly not because there is evidence contrary to Latter-day Saint claims, but it is that the evidence for such claims is not necessarily more compelling than the evidence for their own theological beliefs.

The evidence for the Book of Mormon and Joseph Smith's prophetic calling is, however, if studied objectively, compelling for any honest investigator, and it is of monumental importance to all seekers of spiritual truth. John 17:3 tells us that "this is life eternal, that they might know thee the only true God, and Jesus Christ, who thou hast sent." Believing this, Christians ignore at their peril any additional scripture or revelation that can offer them a fuller understanding of our Heavenly Father and His son Jesus Christ. The scriptures are replete with the lessons learned, often too late, by those who didn't heed the words of prophets. As Abraham said to the rich man who finally, after his death, understood the Plan of Salvation and wanted Lazarus to return and warn his brethren, "If they hear not Moses and the Prophets, neither will they be persuaded though one rose from the dead." How tragic that there will be many who, through prejudice or lack of concern, will hear not the Latter-day prophet Joseph as the rich man heard not Moses and the prophets of his day.

As Jesus started gathering His disciples, soon after His baptism by John, many whom he encountered and attempted to bring into the fold were obviously skeptical. One of these was Nathanael, whom many scholars believe to have been Bartholomew, the apostle. When Philip, who knew Jesus was the Messiah, searched out Nathanael to give him the good news of finding Him of whom Moses and the prophets had written,

Nathanael, the guileless Israelite, questioned Philip. How could the Messiah, for whom they had been waiting all these years, come from such a nondescript local town as Nazareth, which also had not the best reputation for morals and religion? It was to be Nazareth, also, where Jesus was to discover so much hostility in His ministry. After a reading in the synagogue at Nazareth, when Jesus applied the Messianic words of Isaiah to Himself, the people attempted to kill Him.

He was also rejected a second time at Nazareth when the congregation in the synagogue referred disdainfully to His parents and siblings, who were merely their undistinguished neighbors. It was at this time He made the observation that "a prophet is not without honour, but in his own country . . . And he marveled because of their unbelief" (Mark 6:4-6).

It's difficult not to see the parallel between the reception Jesus received in Nazareth and from His countrymen and the reception the Prophet Joseph received in Palmyra and from his countrymen. What Jesus preached, according to many in and around Nazareth, was nothing less than blasphemy. To suggest that He was the Messiah should merit Him nothing less than condemnation, and if that failed, death. What Joseph preached in suggesting he was a prophet chosen by the Lord would merit him condemnation for such blasphemy, and also death. Like Christ, however, the Prophet had his followers who would respond to skeptics as Philip responded to Nathanael when asked if anything good could come out of Nazareth. Philip merely said, "Come and see." This is all that those who accept Joseph as the instrument in the Restoration of the Gospel of Jesus Christ can say to those who question whether such a prophet could have come out of Palmyra; COME AND SEE. It is important, however, that those who desire to know the truth must be as guileless as Nathanael and as discerning as Philip.

INTRODUCTION

Joseph, ceaselessly under attack as a false prophet, was mindful of his inability to categorically "prove" his prophetic calling. In a *Times and Seasons* editorial in September 1842, Joseph prophesied that it would be by circumstantial evidence that the world would prove him to be a true prophet. (*Times & Seasons*, Sept. 15, 1842, 3:922).

As a convert, I was delighted to find that editorial and understood exactly what Joseph was telling his people. Too often we are impressed with the story of Joseph's first vision in which there seems to be an immediate answer to a young boy's prayer. It is common practice for proselytizing Elders, soon after their first meeting with investigators to present them with a *Book of Mormon*, telling them to read it and pray and the Holy Ghost will confirm the truth of the Book and the things the Elders have been telling them. Without doubt, it can and often does happen in this manner, but in many cases, as Joseph apparently realized, it does not. As a convert myself, who has worked with numerous other converts in my three and one half decades in the Church, I can testify, that so many potentially great investigators either will not read the *Book of Mormon* at the Elders' request or they will not pray about it or they will not pray with real intent having the faith essential for an answer. Joseph understood this and that was the reason for his use of the term "circumstantial evidence". He knew that in so many cases, one must get the attention of the investigator and it is by "circumstantial evidence" that that is accomplished.

It too often happens that when an investigator fails to receive an "answer" as they are told Joseph received his, the investigator turns away - convinced that the answer must be negative. Perhaps we should emphasize to such seekers the story of Brigham Young's conversion. It took him nearly two years from his first contact with the *Book of Mormon* before he was convinced of its truth. What was he waiting for? An answer from the Holy Ghost? We can be quite sure he prayed about it and we can be equally sure the Holy Ghost could have confirmed it, but it didn't happen that way. Brigham later said, "I watched to see whether good common sense was manifest." (JD 26:38) That is "circumstantial evidence," pure and simple. If a Prophet of the Lord is led to the ultimate truth by way of circumstantial evidence, then perhaps we should give it more consideration in the Church.

The recent incorporation of F.A.R.M.S. into the Church University should suggest that the time has now arrived when "circumstantial evidence," which is the very purpose for the Foundation for Ancient Research and Mormon Studies, has become in the Church what Joseph Smith envisioned.

It is therefore, for the purpose of further nourishing the fulfillment of that prophesy, that I have assembled several observations concerning fraudulent behavior as normally practiced by those who intend to successfully deceive their fellow beings. If Joseph Smith had such intentions in mind, then he violated every logical aspect of deceptive conduct. Such gross errors of judgment in deceptive behavior can be explained only by sheer stupidity or by divine guidance. Since even his harshest critics have never accused the Prophet Joseph of stupidity, then we must, if such observations are credible, acknowledge the extreme improbability of fraud in the "prophetic calling" of Joseph Smith. One historian writing about Joseph more than twenty years ago stated that he could not understand why Joseph did certain things when "reason alone" should have dictated caution (Porter & Black, p. 281). If reason alone was the guideline for Joseph, he would have done many things differently. That is what this book is all about: to suggest that his failure to follow "reason alone," as an intelligent impostor would have done, is evidence of his prophetic calling.

The twelve patterns of fraudulent behavior described in this book, which the

Prophet Joseph "should" have followed but didn't, are not offered as definitive proof of his divine mission. Such proof can come only as a result of one's own study and prayers and a resulting testimony by the Holy Ghost. They are presented, however, to the convincing of skeptics or investigators that Joseph's short life as an instrument in restoring the Gospel of Jesus Christ bore none of the characteristics of fraudulent behavior.

It is at times ironic that in a Church so dedicated to learning (see chapter 7), sincere believers will scoff at attempts to offer secular evidence to support the authenticity of the *Book of Mormon* or the prophetic calling of the Prophet Joseph, when that is the very reason for the existence of such groups as the Foundation for Ancient Research & Mormon Studies and such symposiums as the Sidney B. Sperry Symposiums at BYU. It was at just such a symposium in 1995 that John W. Welch presented a paper entitled *The Power of Evidence in the Nurturing of Faith.* As long as the evidence adheres to facts, it can be vital, as Welch points out, in facilitating belief.

During the trial of the British soldiers involved in the infamous Boston Massacre the soldiers' defense attorney, John Adams, made the following observation: "Whatever may be our wishes, our inclinations, or the dictates of our passions, they cannot alter the state of facts and evidence."

So it is with the facts supporting the evidence of Joseph Smith's Prophetic calling. The "proof" of such a calling can be no more definitive than that of Moses or any of the other Prophets of Christianity, but they can be just as compelling. The "facts" presented in this book are just that - facts. But the facts, to seekers of the truth, should provide compelling evidence that Joseph Smith was indeed a prophet as he testified.

If he were not a prophet, well-established patterns of known fraudulent behavior would have been evident in the restoration of the church organized by Joseph and his followers. The evidence is overwhelming that almost every act performed by Joseph in the Restoration runs counter to what should be anticipated in the acts of an impostor. So, if fraud had been his intention, what would he have done differently?

CHAPTER I

WOULD HAVE ESTABLISHED THE CHURCH BY REVELATION ONLY

The question is how shall we know
when the things they have spoken
were said as they were 'moved upon
by the Holy Ghost?'
J. Reuben Clark, Jr.

Most major faiths, with identifiable founders, were based not on physical or scriptural finds or actual appearances by spiritual beings, but on a far more incontrovertible claim of revelation. Introducing a "new" faith involving the actual appearances of Biblical personages and a complex thousand-year epic, as in the Book of Mormon, introduces an extremely high risk of exposure if such new teachings are not true.

Joseph Smith lived at a time when interest in exotic places and religions was widespread and magazines and newspapers contained many articles on such subjects. Was Joseph knowledgeable about these topics? His lack of formal schooling has often been mentioned by his critics in a derogatory way and by his supporters as evidence that such an unschooled youth could not have written the Book of Mormon on his own. Even his wife made reference to his lack of education and probably for the same reason when she said in her "last testimony" in 1879:

> Joseph Smith could neither write nor dictate
> a coherent and well-worded letter; let alone
> dictating a book like the Book of Mormon.
> And, though I was an active participant in
> the scenes that transpired, and was present

during the translation of the plates, and had
cognizance of things as they transpired, it is
marvelous to me, "a marvel and a wonder,'"
as much so as to any one else. (BYU Studies,
Vol. 30, No. 1)

It must be remembered, however, that Emma had far more schooling than Joseph – even having spent some time at a private girls' school (Newell & Avery, p.4). In contrast to her own education, Joseph would have seemed much less knowledgeable to his wife.

But certainly Joseph had not grown up in a home devoid of interest in education or the acquisition of knowledge. It must be remembered that his father had taught school in Sharon, Vermont, and would certainly have been interested in imparting knowledge of the world to his children, and obviously had the ability to do so as they labored together on their farm in Palmyra.

Around 1875 Joseph's brother William wrote some notes in response to a critical article on Joseph in *Chambers Miscelany*. In those extensive notes, William, who certainly was better acquainted with his brother than most writers of the time, stated, referring to Joseph's youth, "That he was illiterate to some extent is admitted but that he was enterly (entirely) unlettered is a mistake. In Sintax, authography (orthography)(,) Mathamatics (,) grammar (,) geography with other studies in the common schools of his day he was no novis" (Vogel, p.486).

Joseph, though perhaps deficient in formal education, was undoubtedly well aware of other faiths and their doctrines; certainly more than the average young man today. According to Orson Hyde, Joseph "discovered the religious world laboring under a multitude of errors, which through their contradictory opinions and principles had laid the foundation for the organization of different sects and denominates" (Vogel, p.162). Although such statements about Joseph's confusion over competing sects is usually interpreted as referring to the churches in the immediate vicinity of Palmyra, there is every reason to believe he was talking about the religious "world" as Hyde indicated.

Palmyra was a highly literate community while Joseph was growing up there. Five miles south of the Smith farm was the well-stocked Manchester library, organized around 1812, while only two miles north in Palmyra were several bookstores and at least one library. Starting as early as 1819, book auctions were held in Palmyra, so it is obvious there were well-read people in the community. Although there is little evidence that either Joseph or his hard-working family made much use of these libraries or bookstores, Joseph, as a sociable and intellectually curious youth, had contact with those who were well read (*BYU Studies*, Summer, 1982, pp.333-56). And what were Joseph's well-read neighbors reading at this time? Although books of fiction were beginning to become one of the more popular subjects as the nineteenth century progressed, three of the most dominant subjects in the first two decades were still theology, history and biography (Givens, pp. 258-59), subjects that commonly addressed the topics of world faiths as did periodicals and newspapers of the time. The textbook, *Popular Technology*, published only a decade after the organization of the Mormon Church, noted that "all Europe, with its 200,000,000 of inhabitants, does not support as many regular publications as the United States, with its 17,000.000" (Givens, p.263). Living in such a literate country and community, Joseph's inquisitive mind and interest in religion made him, without doubt, at least somewhat familiar with the founding of such successful world religions as

3

Buddhism and Islam, major faiths based primarily on the revelatory claims of their founders. Buddha, founder of one of the world's great religions, began this Far Eastern faith as a result of a night spent in solitude under a Bo tree, receiving what he considered "enlightenment" on the mysteries of life. No witnesses to any manifestations or evidence of anything spiritual were present for Buddha's "Awakening." The faith was based merely on the wisdom Buddha gained and preached as a result of a night spent in meditation. Although quite remote from the original teachings of Christianity, which Joseph was destined to restore, Buddhism was nevertheless a very visible proof of the possibility of founding a major religion as a consequence of nothing more daring than meditations and resulting enlightenment. Add to this the charisma of a persuasive expounder, something which contemporaries claimed Joseph to be, and a new faith without all the chancy trappings of Mormonism would have been a far more inviting plan of religious deception than the one actually followed by the Prophet Joseph. Critics must at sometime address the question of why Joseph passed up such obviously safer and already proven routes to founding a "new" religion.

Of the world's major faiths, Mormonism is often compared to Islam and Joseph is compared to Mohammed. Aside from the original practice of polygamy and the desire of nineteenth-century critics to impose such an unfavorable foreign image on the Latter-day Saints, there actually is a rather striking comparison. At its very inception, Islam accepted the validity of Judaism and Christianity, as far as they went. Mohammed, like Joseph, considered himself no more than a prophet, but essential to a fulfillment of the work begun by such prophets as Abraham and Moses. He now offered the final truth, completing what the others had begun. Mohammed, like Joseph, was also disturbed by religious perceptions

4

in his culture, specifically one of polytheism. After retiring to a small cave in the mountains north of Mecca to contemplate and pray for a solution to his perplexities just as Joseph did in the Sacred Grove, Mohammed received his answers.

The answers came in a vision when an angel, whom he identified as Gabriel, commanded him to "Proclaim" social justice and monotheism. Emerging from the cave, he began to teach what he had learned and thus began the great religion of Islam. Over the next twenty-three years he received numerous revelations, later compiled into the *Koran*, Islam's holy book. Some of his revelations were received in the presence of others, but none of his associates were witness to the actual visitations of heavenly messengers as was the case with several of Joseph Smith's associates. And having accomplished such a major feat in establishing a world religion primarily through visions and dreams, the opportunity for similar success in a like manner would certainly not have escaped Joseph. But again he ignored such a "proven" and safe course and proceeded to restore the Gospel in a manner that could be far more likely and easily challenged. The only explanation for such illogical behavior is that the Lord's ways are not man's ways and certainly not the ways of a religious fraud.

Actually, it wasn't even necessary to receive revelations in order to found a new religion. Confucianism was founded simply on the strength of the teachings of Confucius concerning ethics, government, and personal goals. It may be argued that Confucianism is not really a religion at all but more of a philosophy. Nevertheless, it is normally classified as a major world religion, one with which Joseph Smith was certainly familiar. And surely he was aware that this major faith originated entirely devoid of any connections with the miraculous or preternatural. Such a highly popular world faith would have appeared a much safer route than the untested route followed by Joseph – if immunity from risk had been a major concern.

There is little question that all of the complexities of the Restoration Gospel made not only a unique addition to the Revivalist impulse of the early nineteenth century, but was also the most demanding for the innovator. If fraudulent, it was without question the most brazen. If the revelatory pattern of establishing a new faith, as in the cases of Islam or Buddhism, might have seemed too challenging to a young man like Joseph Smith, there was certainly an even easier route to take.

The early 1800s were flourishing times for the communitarian impulses in the new nation. More than 100 such communities were founded in America during this time, many of them being widely hailed as successes at the time of Joseph's visit to the Sacred Grove. If the purpose of Joseph's first prayer was to discover the proper route to Christian perfection, the examples were all about him: not to join a traditional Christian sect but to found a community that could withdraw from the world of sectarian bickering.

One of the most dramatically successful American religions previous to Mormonism was the Shakers, and its most vital growth period occurred just as Joseph Smith's revelations were taking place. It had started under the leadership of Mother Ann Lee Stanley in England, but persecution soon forced her and her small band of followers to migrate to America. Believing, as the result of trances and visions, that she was the female incarnation of Jesus, her religion grew rapidly in the revivalist areas, especially among the Baptists. Within ten years of her death in 1784, capable leadership resulted in the building of twelve Shaker communities in New England, and by the time Joseph uttered his prayer in the Grove, several more had been founded in Kentucky, Ohio, and Indiana.

The success of such a religion, based merely on the visions of an illiterate English woman, would certainly have impressed such frontier religious seekers as the Smiths. It would have been demonstrable proof that nothing more than self-claimed revelation was sufficient to create a strikingly acceptable new religion.

A very similar religious communitarian group was the Society of Public Universal Friend, also founded by a woman, Jemima Wilkerson. This group even built a new "Jerusalem" not far from Smith's upstate New York home, where the founder received considerable publicity until she died, about the time Joseph was to enter the Sacred Grove.

Other communities were springing up at this time – the Ephrata and Rappite communities in Pennsylvania, the Zoar community in Ohio, New Harmony by Robert Owen's followers, and dozens more like them. Their seemingly easy successes could not possibly have escaped young Joseph's notice, and if success and recognition had been paramount in Joseph's mind, he would not have ignored such an easy route.

Knowing that such an approach as used by the founders of these faiths is almost impossible to disprove, why, unless his claims were true, would Joseph Smith develop a story with so many complexities that the danger of exposure would be so great? A man, whom even his most vitriolic enemies characterized as "cunning" or "shrewd," would obviously have adopted the least perilous route of faith founding if fraud had been his intention. That he apparently never considered such a course as well as the subsequent failure of all of these communities, would suggest that the claim of Joseph's calling as a Prophet of the

Lord cannot be lightly dismissed.

Today, nearly two thousand years after the beginning of Christianity, critics are still debating the historical accuracy and divine credibility of the Bible. To introduce a new faith with accompanying scriptures, supported with seemingly less historical evidence than the Bible, would appear to be the height of folly, especially when such an endeavor seems totally unnecessary and would logically hinder the acceptance of the "new" faith. The only possible explanation for the introduction of such a detailed and complex chronicle as the Book of Mormon was that Joseph Smith felt completely exempt from dependence on rules of logic as long as truth was his ally.

All of this is not to suggest that other major faiths, founded on the basis of revelation only or predominantly, were fraudulent, but that revelation alone was an entirely sufficient basis for founding some of the world's most successful religions. Why didn't Joseph Smith follow an already tested and proven course?

Joseph was only part of a growing body of religious seekers, most of whom were looking at that time for a restoration of what they referred to as the primitive church of Jesus Christ. To carry out such a "restoration" by a zealous charlatan would require merely recourse to the Bible and pretended revelation to support one's "discoveries." If there was anything in which Joseph was well-versed, it was the Bible. Why, therefore, didn't Joseph follow that simple and practically risk-free route? The answer, of course, is that the decision was not Joseph's. Logical to man or not, it was the Lord's decision.

8

CHAPTER II

WOULD HAVE HAD FEWER WITNESSES

In the mouth of two or three witnesses
shall every word be established.
2 Cor. 13:1

It has always been a widely respected rule of law and theology that any claim could be proven by the testimony of two or more witnesses.. This same theological rule was carried over into the common law of England. Joseph Smith was familiar with and respected this caveat, often carrying it to the extreme by involving a host of witnesses to substantiate his encounters with heavenly beings and revelations. Milton Backman, Professor Emeritus of Church History and Doctrine at Brigham Young University, noted that a variety of witnesses, "unlike any others in religious history, verified Joseph Smith's religious experiences, from the existence of the Book of Mormon plates to the restoration of the Priesthood" (Black, pp.95-96).

The spread of Islam proved, for example, that it was possible to successfully establish a religion with no witnesses to the founder's claims, but Joseph insisted on witnesses to what he had seen and experienced in regard to the original Book of Mormon plates, the keystone of the Restoration.

In late June of 1829, the translation of the plates had revealed the words of Moroni in the fifth chapter of Ether regarding witnesses being granted the privilege of viewing the plates: "And behold, ye may be privileged that ye may show the plates unto those who shall assist to bring forth this work; And unto three shall they be shown by the power of God; wherefore they shall know of a surety that these things are true. And in the mouth of three witnesses shall these things be established." (Ether, 5:2-4).

9

After reading these words, Martin Harris, David Whitmer, and Oliver Cowdery asked Joseph to inquire of the Lord if they might be the three witnesses. Joseph inquired of the Lord and received a revelation directed at Martin, David, and Oliver. The revelation promised that by their faith they would be privileged to view the plates after which time they must testify of them. A few days later the four men, including Joseph, retired into a piece of woods convenient to the Whitmer home. There, after much prayer, they were visited by an angel and shown the plates. According to Joseph's mother, the four men returned to the Whitmer home about mid-afternoon. There, Joseph threw himself down on the bed, exclaiming, "Father! Mother! You do not know how happy I am. The Lord has caused the plates to be shown to three more besides me. They . . . will have to testify to the truth of what I have said . . . it does rejoice my soul that I am not any longer to be entirely alone in the world" (Proctor & Proctor, p.199).

Later, the Prophet, accompanied by several of the Whitmers and Hiram Page, traveled from the Whitmer home in Fayette to the Smith home in Palmyra to make arrangements for having the Book of Mormon printed. Shortly after their arrival in Palmyra, Joseph received permission from the Lord to allow this group plus members of Joseph's family, to be additional witnesses. Records appear to be silent as to what prompted this second viewing, but we do have the signed testimony of four more members of the Whitmer family, Hiram Page, Joseph's father, and two of his brothers, Hyrum and Samuel, that they did indeed see the plates. Retiring to a place in the woods near the Smith home, the plates were shown to these witnesses by the Prophet and they were allowed to handle them and examine the engravings thereon.

Why, after successfully receiving his three witnesses, would Joseph have increased his chances for exposure by involving eight more witnesses, unless he was supremely confident in their recognition of the authenticity of what they had seen? No matter how impressive a fraud it might have been, every additional witness would multiply the risk of exposure at the time of the deceit or would multiply the number who would be able to later testify against him in the event of a "falling out." Actually, of the eleven witnesses, six of them either apostatized from the Church or were excommunicated, but none of them ever denied his testimony of what he had witnessed regarding the original plates. In fact, the original three witnesses renewed their testimony on their deathbeds, which would be rather inconceivable if they had been party to any fraud or even aware of it. A psychological knowledge of deathbed confessions commonly reveals that when facing death, individuals are moved with an urge to set themselves right in meeting their creator. If they have been involved in fraudulent behavior, they will confess and call on God to forgive them. All eleven Book of Mormon witnesses carried their testimonies to their graves. This fact is a remarkable substantiation of what they had witnessed and totally inconsistent with deceitful conspiracies.

This fact is also incompatible to collusive relationships gone sour. To suggest that of six embittered witnesses, not one would deny that Joseph was a prophet is incomprehensible, if such had been the case. Even less understandable is why, assuming their sure knowledge of the prophetic calling of Joseph Smith, at least one didn't bear false witness against Joseph as a retribution for their excommunication. Apparently, all the witnesses had been so deeply impressed by their spiritual experiences that none dared mock the Lord by bearing false witness to what they knew to be true – they had seen the plates and knew the Book of Mormon was true.

Such facts, of course, explain why the witnesses all remained true to their testimony, but it still doesn't explain why Joseph decided he needed eight additional witnesses after successfully acquiring the first three. The answer of course is that Joseph didn't decide – the Lord decided, being well aware of future events regarding the type of criticism that would be leveled at those who claimed to have witnessed the original plates. The Lord knew that two kinds of witnesses would be required to confound the critics.

The first three witnesses, Oliver Cowdery, Martin Harris, and David Whitmer, were observers "only" of a Heavenly personage who handled the plates in front of them. This type of testimony opened them to charges of mental hallucination, as unlikely as it was but nevertheless logical to die-hard critics. As a matter of fact, when an army officer informed David Whitmer years later that he had suffered an hallucination that caused him to think he saw an angel and plates, Whitmer replied emphatically that he "was not under any hallucination," nor was he "deceived." "I know whereof I speak," he asserted (Backman, *Eyewitness Accounts of the Restoration,* p.139).

Such charges might have been easier to make stick if not for the testimony of the second set of witnesses. These eight additional witnesses actually handled the plates, lifting them and turning the pages. Such physical handling of tangible objects by so many individuals certainly served to dissuade critics from further charges of delusion or hallucination.

On the other hand, the demonstration of divine power shown to the first three witnesses would rule out charges that the only witnesses the Prophet could present to the world were those who had been deceived by plates the Prophet had manufactured himself. As improbable as this latter possibility, considering the difficulties faced by an unskilled and poor farmer such as Joseph Smith in crafting a set of plates authentic looking enough to fool eight intelligent individuals, the Lord wished to provide proof sufficient to satisfy any earthly tribunal. Providing both kinds of witnesses was certainly in keeping with the omniscience of the Lord, but a highly unlikely ploy by any individual intent on fraud. Such a person would have been satisfied with his success in obtaining the first three witnesses. It must be pointed out, however, that anyone intent on fraud would probably have avoided looking for witnesses altogether. A successful magician is successful only as long as he can deny his audience an intimate examination of his delusion. The Lord had not only provided witnesses to a heavenly manifestation, but with the Lord's help, Joseph had provided an intimate examination of the plates to a larger audience of eight attesters in broad daylight. An army of sleuths would search the annals of fakery and duplicity in vain to find a comparably successful "delusion." Perhaps that is the reason critics of the Restored Gospel steer so wide of the two sets of testimony found in every *Book of Mormon*.

CHAPTER III

WOULD HAVE INDULGED HIS ASSOCIATES AND FRIENDS

It is better to be deceived by
one's friends than to deceive them.
Goethe

One of the most compelling determinants of an imposture is the endeavor of the "impostor" to involve as few others as possible and to treat with care any associates who are involved. The surest way to be exposed as a fraud is to make enemies of those who are a part of your deception. Nothing is more certain than that disaffected associates of a fraud, especially if public opinion is on their side, will not hesitate to reveal everything about the hoax of which they were once a part. Whether to gain self acclaim for themselves or to relieve a guilty conscience or to get "even" for perceived shabby treatment by former conspirators, it is human nature to "expose" fraud when one is no longer a part of it.

When one considers the comprehensiveness of the Restored Gospel, it becomes inconceivable to imagine a fraud so complex that it could have been worked out without the aid of fellow "conspirators." The Restored Church required the introduction of a sophisticated new scripture based on an ancient manuscript, extensive and detailed doctrines and a complex church organization, all stretching over a period of two decades. The very presence of even one fellow "conspirator" in such an elaborate hoax would have been risking exposure if the associate found little profit in continuing the relationship. Add several "conspirators," which would have been required in such an undertaking, and the risk would have been several times greater. But then to increase the risk several fold by publicly chastising and embarrassing the fellow-conspirators would have been the epitome of witlessness – certainly a charge that Joseph's severest critics have, for the sake of lending credence to their own charges of shrewdness on the part of the Prophet, never leveled. Even Harold Bloom, Jewish author of *The American Religion*, who devoted considerable space in his 1992 bestseller to Mormonism, referred to Joseph Smith as "an authentic religious genius" (p.82). A genius is certainly not someone who would disregard the risks and jeopardize such a grand deception by purposely and publicly censuring and deprecating his fellow conspirators.

And yet from the very beginning of his calling as a Prophet, Joseph never hesitated to criticize or chastise intimates he felt were deserving of reprimand. He consistently corrected other speakers who preceded him in public discourses and usually in a blunt manner. Most revealing, however, in his disinclination to pamper misguided or misinformed followers, was his custom of seeking the Lord's counsel regarding associates, and publicly revealing that information, whether commendable or critical. The Lord, through Joseph, identifies by name in the Doctrine and Covenants, 130 contemporary associates of the Prophet. Many of these are blessings or instructions regarding missions and so forth, but many are also embarrassingly critical of the associates and friends mentioned.

The sacrifices of some of Joseph's closest associates did not exempt them from these public criticisms. In March of 1829 at Harmony, Pennsylvania, and at the request of Martin Harris himself, Joseph received a revelation from the Lord that is now Section 5 of the D&C. Martin Harris, as stated earlier, was one of the original Three Witnesses. He was also a respectable Palmyra farmer who mortgaged his farm to finance the printing of the Book of Mormon and whose association with Joseph eventually cost him that farm, his reputation, and his wife. And yet the revelation received by Joseph on that day in 1829 warned

15

Martin that "Yea, I foresee that if my servant Martin Harris humbleth not himself and receive a witness from my hand, that he will fall into transgression." An even more devastating criticism was made public the previous year after Martin was responsible for losing the 116 manuscript pages from the translation of the "Book of Lehi." In that revelation, now Section 10 of the D&C, Martin is referred to as "a wicked man."

Frederick G. Williams was a member of the First Presidency who was excommunicated but later came back into the Church and died in the faith. In 1833, before his excommunication, he was publicly chastised in a revelation received by Joseph in Kirkland, Ohio. As recorded in section 93 of the D&C, the Lord told Williams, "You have not taught your children light and truth, according to the commandments; that wicked one hath power, as yet, over you, and this is the cause of your affliction." In the same revelation, the Lord, through the Prophet Joseph, chastises one of Joseph's closest and most trusted associates, Sidney Rigdon: "Verily I say unto my servant Sidney Rigdon, that in some things he hath not kept the commandments concerning his children; therefore, first set in order thy house" (D&C 93:44). Only six verses later, Joseph's good friend Newel K. Whitney, who was at the time providing Joseph and his family with a home, came under condemnation: "My servant Newel K. Whitney also, a bishop of my church, hath need to be chastened, and set in order his family, and see that they are more diligent and concerned at home, and pray always, or they shall be removed out of their place" (D&C, 93:50). Bishop Whitney humbly accepted the chastisement and remained a friend and strong in the Church.

It is of interest to note that the same revelation refers to Joseph himself as not having kept the commandments, and instructs that he "must needs stand rebuked before the Lord" (D&C 93:47). Joseph's own chastisement must stand as further evidence of his calling. A fraudulent leader would never say "The Lord is unhappy with me or my work as a prophet." Such a leader would want to always be able to put himself above his people as the epitome of divine perfection or at least as someone so worthy of his position that the Lord would never need to rebuke him. People are always more willing to follow an infallible religious leader.

Other examples of the Prophet chastising his associates are found in section 124 of the D&C concerning Almon Babbitt, who was President of the Kirkland Stake from 1841 to 1843. He held a number of other important positions in Church and government, including one as unseated delegate to Congress from Utah. When he was killed by Indians around 1856, he was still faithful in the Church, despite the revelation given fifteen years earlier that stated, "And with my servant Almon Babbitt, there are many things with which I am not pleased," referring to the setting up of "a golden calf for the worship of my people" (D&C 124:84), a rather serious charge and one not likely to be easily forgotten by men less sure of Joseph's authority as a prophet.

And in that same revelation, Joseph, again as spokesman for the Lord, turns his attention to another close associate, Robert D. Foster: "And let him repent of all his folly, and clothe himself with charity; and cease to do evil, and lay aside all his hard speeches" (D&C 124:116). Certainly Foster, a known womanizer, deserved the reprimand, but for that public criticism, Joseph was to later be rewarded when Foster became one of the leading protagonists in the campaign against Joseph in his final days in Nauvoo..

There are numerous other examples throughout the Doctrine and

Covenants in which hardworking and seemingly faithful and respected associates of Joseph Smith are censured. This is certainly not recommended practice for any impostor who must be fearful at all times of exposure, especially by disaffected disciples. This was apparently of little concern to Joseph who knew there was no fraud to be revealed but that what he was doing was out of love: "I frequently rebuke and admonish my brethren, and that because I Love them, not because I wish to incur their displeasure, or mar their happiness. Such a course of conduct is not calculated to gain the good will of all, but rather the ill will of many; . . . but rebukes and admonitions become necessary, from the perverseness of the brethren, for their temporal as well as spiritual welfare" (Smith, J. Fielding, pp. 112-13).

Joseph's unwillingness to indulge contemporaries when they erred was not limited to just his associates in the Church. Joseph did have friends of influence outside the Church, but this did not prevent him from speaking frankly to such acquaintances when he felt they deserved frankness, even though it might offend them.

One such individual was James A. Bennet, an influential attorney and proprietor and principal of the Arlington House, an educational institution on Long Island. Actually, there is some evidence that he may have been baptized by Brigham Young in New York, but Bennet never really considered himself a member nor was he ever considered a member in good standing. When he wrote to Joseph Smith on October 24, 1843, with lavish praise and concluding with a promise to buy land in Illinois and to work in Joseph's behalf, he ended the letter by saying, "I expect to be yet, through your influence, governor of the state of Illinois." Joseph replied on November 13 from Nauvoo asking if he should

18

"worm himself into a political hypocrite" or "stoop from the sublime authority of Almighty God to be handled as a monkey's cat-paw, and pettify myself into a clown to act the farce of political demagoguery?" (HC, 6:78).

Joseph's unfriendly response apparently aroused no antagonism in Bennet, who, after the Prophet's death, offered his services to Brigham Young. When the Utah leadership failed to respond, the New Yorker turned to the Reorganized Church with an offer of support in the "Reformation of Mormon practice" (BYU Studies, Vol.19, No.2, p.249).

Only a man of God, supremely confident of his calling, would risk losing the friendship of such an influential person when it would have seemed so beneficial to have offered Mr. Bennet his support in exchange for further favorable publicity, which Bennet had extended to the Saints previously and which they still needed so badly.

CHAPTER IV

WOULD HAVE BEEN ACCUSED BY APOSTATES OF FRAUD – NOT OF HAVING "FALLEN"

*Histories are more full of examples
of the fidelity of dogs than of friends.*
Alexander Pope

It was May 3, 1844 – only seven weeks before Joseph's martyrdom – and Brigham Young was writing from his home to a mission leader in England about the state of affairs in Nauvoo. In the last paragraph of his long letter he was warning Elder Hedlock about the possibility of some apostates showing up in England doing missionary work for an apostate church:

> William and Wilson Law, Robert D. Foster, Chauncey L. and
> Francis Higbee, Father Cowles, &c., have organized a new
> church. (Laws and Fosters were first cut off.) William Law is
> Prophet; James Blakesley and Cowles, Counselors; Higbee and
> Foster of the Twelve. Cannot learn all particulars. Charles Ivins,
> Bishop; old Dr. Green and old John Scott, his counselors. They
> are talking of sending a mission to England, but it will probably
> be after this when they come among you. 'Tis the same old story
> over again – "The doctrine is right, but Joseph is a fallen prophet"
> (HC, 6:354).

The dark forces of apostasy and anti-Mormonism were daily gathering strength in and around Nauvoo and the Prophet Joseph Smith. The greatest threat as seen by the Latter-day Saints, however, was not the anti-Mormons, as numerous and powerful as they were. The Saints had experienced the ultimate in persecution by this group only six years previously – forcible expulsion under

20

threat of extermination from the neighboring state of Missouri. But it was those within the community and Church who were creating the greatest problems for Joseph – men who once held positions of respect and authority in city government and Church leadership positions. Now, for a variety of reasons, some of them doctrinal and others personal, these disaffected individuals were allying themselves with the growing number of anti-Mormons in Illinois who believed Joseph Smith was a false prophet.

But the difference between these two groups of antagonists was that the enemies outside the Church viewed Joseph as a false prophet while the apostate group of the Laws, Fosters, the Higbees, and others considered Joseph a "fallen" prophet. The distinction is important. Those who had known Joseph most intimately, but whose animosity now appeared the greater, still recognized his original prophetic calling, even wishing to continue the church Joseph was responsible for restoring. The letter Brigham Young wrote to Elder Hedlock was prompted by a meeting of the apostates at Wilson Law's during which the group had voted to replace Joseph and other leaders because the prophet was "fallen."

In fact, when the disaffected group concocted a plan to expose their "fallen" prophet by publishing an opposition newspaper in Nauvoo called the *Nauvoo Expositor*, their first and only issue affirmed the group's beliefs in the Book of Mormon and the Doctrine and Covenants. It was the destruction of this newspaper as a "public nuisance" by official order of the Nauvoo city council that resulted in the arrest of Joseph and his death at the hands of a Carthage mob. This mob included some of the very same apostates who still did not deny Joseph's prophetic calling. In fact, on the front page of the first and only issue, they printed, "We all verily believe and many of us know of a surety that the religion of the Latter Day Saints, as originally taught by Joseph Smith, which is contained in the Old and New Testaments, Book of Covenants, and Book of Mormon, is verily true; and that the pure principles set forth in those books, are the immutable and eternal principles of Heaven," (*Nauvoo Expositor*, p.1).

To have joined the anti-Mormon forces in calling Joseph a false prophet would certainly have made the apostate group more acceptable and credible to the Church enemies they turned to for help in disposing of Joseph and other Church leaders. The fact that even their vile hatred of Joseph could not persuade them to denounce Joseph as a "false" prophet should create some degree of doubt in the minds of anyone who believes Joseph Smith's claim of Prophetic calling was fraudulent. It is of interest that even today the most extreme critics of the Latter-day Saints, in an effort to destroy the credibility of Joseph Smith as a prophet of the Restored Gospel, still distribute copies of the *Nauvoo Expositor*, which verifies his prophetic calling.

The Prophet was well aware of the significance of the refusal of the most savage defectors to classify him as a false prophet. In a public address in Nauvoo only six weeks before his death in the Carthage jail, Joseph asserted, "My enemies say that I have been a true prophet. Why, I had rather be a fallen prophet than a false prophet" (HC, 6:364).

After Joseph's death, an increase in apostasy occurred as some members sought new leadership, and others, tired of persecution and uncertain of the future of the Church, left its ranks. A large number of the apostates who rejected the leadership of the Council of Twelve took up the cry of "fallen" prophet as justification for their desertion from the main body of the church. During those dark months following the martyrdoms, however, there appeared to be few defectors who felt they had been deceived by a "false" leader.

In fact, leaders such as Brigham Young appeared to be much more concerned about those who believed Joseph had "fallen." At an 1844 conference of the Church held in Nauvoo in October following Joseph's death, Brigham said, "It is the test of our fellowship to believe and confess that Joseph lived and died a Prophet in good standing; and I don't want anyone to fellowship the Twelve who says Joseph is fallen" (HC, 7:287-88). There was an obvious lack of concern about any charges of "false" prophet, indicating a rather universal belief among members and apostates alike that a true church had been restored and that Joseph had been the prophet chosen to lead it.

Ironically, one of the reasons the apostates gave for believing Joseph had fallen was their charge that he had made mistakes in the selection of unworthy associates, possibly an unconscious reference to themselves. It is almost a paradox, also, that some of the most demonstrable proofs of Joseph Smith's prophetic calling were to result from the apostasy of some of these, perhaps unwisely chosen associates, who held such vital positions in the First Quorum of the Twelve, in the First Presidency, and even as original witnesses. If the general apostasies in Ohio, Missouri, and Illinois had been limited primarily to lesser members, not as well acquainted with Joseph, charges of Joseph being a false prophet might well have been more widespread and effective. Ironically, however, it was because of the presence of the more notable original witnesses and intimate associates among the apostates, men who were best qualified to judge the prophetic calling of Joseph and the authenticity of the Book of Mormon, refusing to charge Joseph as a "false" prophet that lesser members were

23

discouraged from making such charges. As a result, it was almost impossible for enemies outside the Church to find deserters who would verify their claims that Joseph had fraudulently organized the church and devised a new set of scriptures to accompany it. Even the occasional insignificant apostate who might make such a charge would be ignored or his charges overshadowed by the important and better known apostates who, even in their hostility toward Joseph, recognized and admitted his prophetic calling. Their disaffection was less understandable and certainly less convincing to Church enemies than the allegation that the Church had been fraudulently established. This would continue to be a perplexing problem to the enemies outside the Church who never did quite understand. Why did disaffected members not accuse Joseph of being a "false" prophet? This would continue to be a dilemma to outside critics as long as Joseph was alive or there were those alive who had intimately known him. There is no question that those early apostates did damage the Church, but only because the average non-Mormon was not perceptive enough to recognize the difference between "false" and "fallen," or did not even notice the reasons for the apostasies. They were merely cheered to see "drop-outs" from a religion the media had taught them to despise, or to hear any accusation against the Mormon prophet, even though those accusations might ingeniously validate his prophetic calling.

When Joseph said that he would rather have been accused of "fallen" than false, it must be acknowledged by his most severe critics that the term "false" would certainly have been a far more serious indictment. And it must also be acknowledged that the most vitriolic of enemies are those who turn against former friends and associates. Rational thought must therefore recognize that if belief of fraud had been present in the minds of his most malevolent class of enemies, it would have been demonstrated when they turned against the Prophet and the Church. The fact that it was not should indeed be powerful confirmation of the Prophet Joseph Smith's calling as a restorer of the Church of Jesus Christ.

CHAPTER V

WOULD HAVE TRIED TO PROFIT FINANCIALLY

> The only principle upon which (my enemies) judge
> me is by comparing my acts with the foolish traditions
> of their fathers and nonsensical teachings of hireling
> priests, whose object and aim were to keep the
> people in ignorance for the sake of filthy lucre.
> - Joseph Smith (HC 5:516-17)

In demonstrating this particular thesis, critics are especially useful. As "proof" that Joseph Smith was a fraud, critics have leveled the charge that Joseph did exactly what this chapter claims he would have done if he had been a fraud – but the fact is he did not.

One of his most vehement critics early in the twentieth century was Theodore Schroeder, who, in an article in the *American Historical Magazine*, wrote that "a desire for money was the inspiring cause of every act of the Mormon Prophet" and that when Joseph was killed, he was "the richest man in Nauvoo" (Roberts, 2:81). Let's investigate to see if such charges have merit, as they should have if Joseph was a fraud as his critics claim.

It was a full eight years after the Church was organized before Joseph approached the High Council at Far West with a request for some compensation for the time he and Sidney Rigdon devoted to Church business at the expense of their families. In the Joseph Smith History of the Church, we find this entry for May 12, 1838: "We (Sidney and Joseph) stated to the Council our situation, as to maintaining our families . . . spending as we have for eight years, our time, talents, and property, in the service of the Church; and being reduced as it were to beggary."

Joseph went on to indicate his willingness to work to support his family if

26

that was what was decided, but if the Church should say, "Serve us," some provision must be made for our sustenance" (HC 3:31-32). The Council thereupon voted compensation for their services, "not for preaching or for receiving the word of God by revelation neither for instructing the Saints in righteousness, but for Services rendered in the printing establishment in translating the ancient records &c. &c." Elder Ebenezer Robinson stated, however, that because of the uproar that followed, the idea of paying the First Presidency annual wages was finally dropped (Cannon & Cook, p.188). It is of interest to discover that two days later, while Sidney is preparing and correcting some matter for the press, Joseph spends the day plowing.

At no time during Joseph's fourteen years as head of the Church did he expect the members to support him or his family merely because of his position as President and Prophet. Such was apparently not in the Prophet's nature. His New England work ethic seemed to demand a more tangible endeavor for benefits than simply a title – a rather curious set of ethics for the impostor his enemies accused him of being. Such ethics, we discover, were sworn to before a magistrate at the Lyons District Court in New York in 1829.

Martin Harris's wife, Lucy, had charged Joseph of fraud with the intent of obtaining money from her husband by claiming to have gold plates. At the trial Martin, a respectable and affluent Palmyra farmer, testified in Joseph's favor against his own wife. Under oath he raised his hand and said, "I can swear, that Joseph Smith never has got one dollar from me by persuasion, since God made me.... This, I can pointedly prove; and I can tell you, furthermore, that I have never seen in Joseph Smith, a disposition to take any man's money, without giving him a reasonable compensation for the same in return" (Smith, Lucy Mack, 1958,

146). After Martin's testimony, the magistrate dismissed the charges.

Wherever Joseph took up residence with his followers, he labored for a living, while at the same time administering to the needs of the thousands who joined the Church and called upon him for spiritual and temporal assistance and advice. In spite of such pressing duties as these and caring for his families, he still made time for missionary work. During the Kirtland era alone, Joseph undertook fourteen proselytizing missions. Between 1831 and 1838 he served a full-time mission at least once each year (*Church History in the Fulness of Times*, p.117). But often, even this work for the Lord had to be temporarily set aside while he labored to provide for his family, usually in farming or storekeeping.

Joseph had grown up on a farm and that seemed to be the work he usually turned to – either for himself or neighbors – in the early days of the Church. New Church members or investigators often mentioned in their journals their first meetings with the Prophet, finding him at work in the fields, claiming no special privilege as prophet or leader of a rapidly expanding church.

One such record keeper was Joseph Noble, who joined the Church in Kirtland and served in numerous Church positions until his death in Utah in 1900: "When I arrived in Kirtland, I went to the house of Joseph Smith and told him I had come to stay a few days in the place. He was going to work in the hayfield. He invited me to go with him . . . I stayed nine days at the place, worked with the prophet six days" (Noble, p.4).

While living in Kirtland and only three weeks before the March of Zion's Camp and in the midst of problems associated with the persecutions in Missouri, Joseph noted in his personal diary for April of 1834 that on Tuesday the 15th, he "drawed a load of hay" and the next day he "plowed and sowed oats for Brother

Frederick (G. Williams)" (Jessee, p.33).

After returning from the Zion's Camp expedition, Joseph became involved in laboring with his own hands in the stone quarry for the new temple. Heber C. Kimball recalled at a talk given in Utah in 1863 that "When we arrived in Kirtland, Joseph said, 'Come, brethren, let us go into the stone quarry and work for the Lord'. And the Prophet went himself, in his tow frock and tow breeches, and worked at quarrying stone like the rest of us" (JD, 10:166).

In May 1839, soon after Joseph had escaped from the authorities in Missouri and had rejoined his family in Quincy, Illinois, he moved with his wife and children to Commerce (later Nauvoo), located north of Quincy along the Mississippi River. Soon after this, Warren Foote, along with some of the male members of his family, also traveled to Commerce from their temporary residence near Quincy. They had fled to that area after their expulsion from Missouri and were looking for a permanent place to settle near Commerce. Brother Foote had been acquainted with the Prophet in Kirtland and was now anxious to see him again. He sought him out at his home in Commerce and found him "busy in clearing off a garden spot, and plowing it" (*Warren Foote Autobiography*, typescript, pp.35-36). Being forced to postpone essential Church work in order to provide for his family seemed to have been a general pattern for the prophet.

Because of the destitute condition of the Saints from repeated losses in their expulsions from Ohio and Missouri, Joseph never seemed comfortable in asking for assistance for his family in spite of his very large legal bills. Still, his followers were not unaware of the needs of the prophet and his family. At the conclusion of a general conference held in the Town of Orange, Cuyahoga County, Ohio, in October 1831, the subject of sending Elders to visit the churches

29

in order to obtain means for the support of Joseph and his family was brought up (*Cannon & Cook*, 23-24). The minutes of the conference do not record the results of this suggestion, but it was obviously a problem throughout the rest of Joseph's life. Years later a Council Meeting of the Twelve Apostles was held at the home of Brigham Young in Nauvoo. The minutes of that meeting record very succinctly the normal financial circumstances of the Prophet and his family:

> Resolved unanimously, that we deeply feel for our beloved President Joseph Smith, and his father's family, on account of the great losses they have sustained in property by the unparalleled persecutions in Missouri, as well as the other many persecutions they have sustained since the rise of the Church, which has brought them to their present destitute situation . . . Therefore, voted unanimously, that we for ourselves, and the Church we represent, approve of the proceedings of President Smith, so far as he has gone, in making over certain properties to his wife, children, and friends for their support. (HC, 4:412-13).

That resolution was passed in 1841, but apparently it was not sufficient for the needs of the Prophet and his family. Ever conscious of possible charges of profiteering, Joseph was reluctant to profit personally from the sale of Nauvoo property when there were so many immigrants with so little money to purchase property. It comes as no surprise then that two years later the Quorum of the Twelve felt it necessary to come to the relief of the Prophet's family. In a letter to Latter-day Saint congregations around Illinois, Brigham Young, president of the Twelve wrote: "He (Joseph) has not provision for himself and family, and is obliged to spend his time in providing thereof. His family is large and his

30

company great, and it requires much to furnish his table. And now, brethren, we call on you for immediate relief in this matter" (HC, 5:293).

In spite of his normal destitute situation, Joseph still did not hesitate to work alongside the Church brethren on public or Church projects. In Nauvoo, as well as Kirtland, Joseph worked in the quarry during the building of the Temple. John Pulsipher, in his autobiography for the year 1842, wrote, "The temple progressed with the Saints that could work at it steady. The Prophet Joseph worked with his own hands, quarrying the stone for its wells when his enemies were not pursuing him" (Pulsipher, p.6). Such hard physical labor is not characteristic of a leader who is attempting to delude his followers with claims of divine privilege.

Joseph's willingness to sacrifice for the Church extended further, however, than to merely his time and labor. His readiness to deny himself or his family available comfort and convenience was far more characteristic of a prophet of the Lord than a self-aggrandizing and deceptive superior. Shortly after the prophet's family established a home in an existing building in the little hamlet of Commerce, newly arriving Saints were felled by the hundreds by Malaria, which they called "swamp fever" or "ague." Hundreds of these new arrivals had no homes to move into and were forced to lay in the open or under make-shift shelters along the river. Emma and Joseph, who at this time had four children of their own, filled their house with the sick and Emma spent countless hours nursing the afflicted with her own medicines. Joseph himself moved into a tent he had pitched in his door yard. Worn out from caring for the sick, the Prophet soon sickened and was forced into bed.

Slowly, as Nauvoo prospered, life became a little easier for Joseph and his family. Only in the last couple of years of his life, however, did he find work that permitted him more time for the increasing duties associated with the rapidly growing church. This occurred in running and finally leasing his Mansion House, a popular rooming house for Nauvoo's many visitors. But even then, visitors to his table, although always welcome and graciously entertained, often spoke of the modest fare. Mosiah Hancock recalled a visit to the Prophet's home in Nauvoo:

> As I glanced on his table and beheld a beautiful boiled
> corn on the cob, I thought "Oh, what a grand sight! The
> corn seemed to be of the King Phillip variety of yellow flint.
> Brother Joseph asked his father to return thanks on the
> food, and Father Smith took up an ear of corn in his right
> hand holding it between his thumb and forefinger, and said,
> "Oh, God, the Eternal Father, we thank thee for this corn,
> and pray in the name of Jesus Christ to bless it to the
> strengthening of our bodies, and the strengthening of our
> stomachs till Thou can provide something better; which
> we ask of Thee in the name of Jesus Christ, Amen."
> Tears were streaming down his cheeks, and I thought
> it a repast of the most excellent type. (Hancock, pp. 14-15)

In addition to enriching themselves, most impostors also use their positions of influence and their profits to reward family and friends. Did Joseph do that or even attempt it?

In July of 1838 Joseph was in Missouri and his youngest brother, Don Carlos, was on his way to join him. On the sixth of that month, Joseph received a letter from his brother who was somewhere in Indiana when he wrote it on his

32

way from Kirkland:

> We were disappointed on every hand before we started
> in getting money. We got no assistance whatever – We
> had, when we started, $75 in money. . . now we have
> only $25 to carry twenty-eight souls and thirteen horses
> five hundred miles . . . Our courage is good, and I think
> we shall be brought through. I leave it with you and
> Hyrum to devise some way to assist us to some more
> money." (HC 3:43)

Almost a year later Don Carlos was living in Nauvoo and desperately searching for a way, along with Ebenezer Robinson, to raise two hundred dollars as a down payment in printing a third edition of the Book of Mormon. They had none themselves but were able to borrow $145 from a brother in the Church (Robinson, p. 258).

What about Hyrum? Did the Prophet's dearest friend and beloved brother fare any better? The records seem to indicate just the opposite. Joseph relied on Hyrum for not only moral and spiritual support, but apparently for what little financial support he might also provide. With no assets, such support had apparently been in the form of pledging future assets as collateral for loans in building up the Church, specifically the Kirtland Temple. Now, in April 1838, Joseph was in Far West preparing to build another Temple, but painfully aware of the burden he and the Lord had been placing on Hyrum. On the 26th of that month, Joseph received a revelation concerning the building of a Temple at Far West, but which also revealed that Hyrum as a member of the First Presidency was not to "get in debt anymore for the building of a house unto my name" (D&C

115:13).

Did any of Joseph's other brothers profit from Joseph's position as Church President? Shortly before Joseph's death, he had his last meeting with his brother William, who asked him at that time for a city lot near the temple. Joseph was willing to give his brother the lot, provided William would build a home on it and live there, to which William agreed. Within a matter of hours, however, a Mr. Ivins checked with the city recorder to make sure the title was clear and actually belonged to Joseph's brother since William had just sold it to him for $500. Upon being notified, Joseph immediately stopped the transfer. This action by the Prophet so enraged William that he threatened Joseph, who discreetly avoided his brother until he shortly thereafter left Nauvoo for the East (Nibley, p.344).

If neither Joseph nor his family were materially profiting from the Church Joseph was credited with restoring, did anyone else? Outside his own family the one closest to Joseph was his most loyal and devoted follower, Brigham Young. Joseph loved Brigham and relied on him for advice and aid in building the Church. If anyone needed financial help, it would certainly have been Brigham, considering the amount of time he spent away from his family on missions. He once noted:

> I took a mission to Canada at my own expense; and
> from the time that I was baptized until the day of our
> sorrow and affliction, at the martyrdom of Joseph and
> Hyrum, no summer passed over my head but what I
> was traveling and preaching, and the only thing I ever
> received from the Church, during over twelve years,
> and the only means that were ever given me by the

34

Prophet, that I now recollect, was in 1842, when

brother Joseph sent me the half of a small pig that

the brethren had brought to him. (JD 4:34)

During that same address, which was given in the Bowery in Salt Lake

City in 1856, he pointedly stated that none of the brethren who were on missions

in the days of Joseph received any help from the Church. And if he had any funds

available himself, "it almost universally went into the hands of brother Joseph, to

pay lawyers' fees and to liberate him from the power of his enemies" (JD 4:34).

Conclusive evidence of Joseph's unwillingness to personally profit from

his position as Church President is found in records of his estate at the time of his

death, directly contradicting the charges of such critics as Schroeder, who

believed that Joseph's "profiteering" was evidence of fraud. Only two years

previous to his martyrdom, Joseph had recorded in his journals that "In

consequence of the utter annihilation of our property by mob violence in the state

of Missouri, and the immense expenses which we were compelled to incur, . . . we

were reduced to the necessity of availing ourselves of the privileges of the general

bankrupt law" (HC, 4:600). Joseph's estate records reveal that not only did he

die without assets, but was actually in debt again.

In February of 1841, a little more than a year after moving to Nauvoo,

Joseph was "vested with plenary powers, as sole Trustee in Trust for the Church

of Jesus Christ of Latter-day Saints, to receive, acquire, manage or convey

property, real, personal, or mixed, for the sole use and benefit of said Church"

(HC 4:287)

The decision to make such an arrangement was not unique to the Church,

nor a desire of Joseph to arrange an opportunity for personal gain. It was a common practice in other churches and organizations and was set up in Nauvoo in accordance with a state statute enacted six years previously.

As trustee-in-trust for the Church, his personal property was easily confused with church property, which fact caused considerable legal confusion as well. An Illinois law declared that no church could hold more than ten acres of property, so the Latter-day Saint's church properties owned in 1846, when Nauvoo was evacuated, was concluded to belong to the trustee-in-trust's widow, Emma, and thus subject to sale to pay off any creditors. And there were plenty of creditors.

When the final claims were filed in 1849, there was a total of thirty-seven equaling more than $25,000, far more than the liquid assets. As Nauvoo was evacuated, all the property the Church was able to find immediate buyers for was sold for pennies on the dollar, and the money had gone into the Church coffers where it rightfully belonged. After the evacuation public auctions were held of the remaining Church lots listed under Joseph's name to satisfy the $25,000 debt. Before the debtors could collect, however, the Federal Government filed claim on all remaining property, including Smith family property, for the debt still owed on the steamship NAUVOO. Eighteen hundred dollars in surplus was finally returned to Emma, but she had to use that plus another thousand of her personal money to buy back the Mansion House, the Nauvoo House, the Homestead, and the farm east of town, all of which had also been sold by the authorities. Everything would have been lost if not for the efforts of her lawyer to salvage something left her by Joseph. It was reported by Edward Tullidge, a contemporary Church historian who wrote a history of the Prophet in 1878, that Joseph's "worldly possessions, probably, never at any time exceeded two or three thousands dollars . . . At his death the administrator could allow the widow only $124 a year from the estate" (Smith & Sjodahl, p.124). Thus it was, that Emma and her new husband were forced to labor hard the rest of their lives to make ends meet (Newell & Avery, 1984, 258-59).

Could Joseph Smith have profited from his position if he had so desired? The answer is obviously yes, considering only the value of the Nauvoo Temple alone, which Joseph insisted had to be constructed. That tremendously expensive edifice absorbed funds and labor that could easily have been diverted to the use of the Church's destitute leader. He could have simply asked for funds to free him for the important Church work of which his many followers had a testimony. In fact, as translator, he could easily have claimed a share of profits from the sale of the *Book of Mormon* – five editions of which were printed during his life. There is no evidence, however, that he ever considered it.

Mary Baker Eddy, on the other hand, founder of the First Church of Christ Scientist, used the royalties from her book, Science and Health, published in 1875, to become a wealthy woman. This is not a criticism of Ms. Eddy, but merely an observation of a legitimate practice of religious leaders. With her first royalties she bought a house in Lynn, Massachusetts, and years later when the Mother Church was built in Boston, she was able to make the biggest donation for its construction. Although extremely generous with her money, she nevertheless led a comfortable life as a result of the sale of the Christian Science scriptures.

We cannot overlook one additional doctrinal tenet that was introduced in the Restored Church – one costly to Joseph personally, but further evidence of a faith managed by the Lord and not Joseph. There would be no paid ministry in the Lord's Church. Permitting a paid clergy would have made life much easier for

Joseph without any resulting criticism, since it was and still is common practice in practically all Christian Churches.

Failure to profit from his leadership position is not necessarily evidence of the prophetic calling of Joseph Smith, but unwillingness to attempt to profit is an indication that a significant characteristic of fraud was not present in Joseph's claims to Prophetic leadership. Any objective observer must recognize Joseph's willingness to live in such an underprivileged and unproperous manner for something he believed in so strongly. If a fraud, then Joseph was his own worst victim.

CHAPTER VI

WOULD HAVE DEVISED DOCTRINES MORE APPEALING TO THE MASSES

To say that man could devise a better organization for
the accomplishment of these several objects would be
to challenge the wisdom of God.
B. H. Roberts

Before Joseph Smith and the Restoration, only a few of the better educated understood the historic need for a restoration of the original Church of Christ. Roger Williams, who left the Baptist Church, which he had founded in the New World, and became a seeker of the primitive Christian Church, and Thomas Jefferson, who did not ally himself with any organized religion because he too was seeking a church closer to the one founded by Christ, are two of the most prominent names that come to mind.

The masses in 1830, for the most part, accepted the traditional religions of their fathers, which meant adhering to such beliefs as a three-in-one trinity; a spiritual, formless God; the traditional concepts of heaven and hell; and so forth. Joseph was immersed in the religious fervor and agitation of the American frontier, but the participants around him were not seeking a new faith; their frenzy and passions were merely demonstrations of new-found zeal in primitive Bible thumping.

If foisting a new religion on his family and frontier acquaintances was his objective, the most reasonable route would have incorporated the conventional and orthodox doctrines already accepted by the masses. It seemed that almost every doctrinal departure from orthodox Protestantism in the Restored Gospel was designed to arouse objections among the conventional heirs of New England

39

Puritanism – the very targets of his missionary aims. It appears that every "new" doctrine in the Restored Church was designed to discourage conversion. There were a few minor religious groups, such as Quakers, Unitarians, and Shakers, who shared some similar beliefs such as salvation for the dead and Biblical errancy (Backman, 1970, 329-50), but none with so many doctrines at odds with the majority of Christians as the LDS Church.

Not only were these doctrines at odds with the religious traditions of those the Mormon missionaries needed to target for conversion, but they seemed, in the Jacksonian period in which they arose, to be anti-democratic and thus anti-American.

Claiming descent from the only true Church of Jesus Christ, the Latter-day Saints seemed to repudiate the Jacksonian concept of social egalitarianism so prevalent in early nineteenth-century America. This heresy, perhaps as much as any single radical doctrinal teaching, infuriated the Saints' neighbors against this subversive alien and anti-American cancer.

Dan Vogel, in his *Religious Seekers and the Advent of Mormonism*, echoes the consensus of many historians when he refers to Mormonism as "a radical, even revolutionary movement, and its theocracy seemed anachronistic, if not subversive, on the American frontier" (217). Vogel refers to the Disciples of Christ as an example of a more typical emerging American faith that attempted to adapt to the democratic impulses of the new republic.

The Disciples of Christ was historically a movement that emerged on the American frontier out of the Great Revivals and previous to the Restoration of the Church of Jesus Christ of Latter-day Saints. It gained widespread popularity under such leaders as Alexander Campbell, who championed democracy by blending

40

the independence of the American frontier (no authority beyond the local congregation) with a restoration of the "ancient order" of the Christian Church (a creedless and uncomplicated biblical faith).

Rather than following such a proven formula, however, Joseph Smith, while restoring the "ancient order," did not adopt the other already proven and popular aspects of the Disciples movement. On the contrary, it seems that the "Restoration" concept was the only tenet of the Mormon Church that was not considered radical in the early nineteenth century.

Let's examine some of these tenets that appeared to be purposely designed to be universally objectionable to nineteenth-century Americans.

ANTHROPOMORPHIC GOD

The first revealed doctrine of the new faith, resulting from Joseph's prayer in the sacred grove, divulged an anthropomorphic Godhead with Jesus and His father as two distinct personages. As logical as such a revelation may have seemed to some of the seekers, it certainly flew in the face of the general Christian concept of a formless and mysterious Trinity. Nearly the entire Christian world, Catholics and Protestants alike, taught that God was a spirit. God as an immaterial being had evolved in the early centuries of the Christian Church, partly as a result of the influence of Neo-Platonic philosophy, which assumed matter was essentially evil. Fitting neatly with the traditional Christian concept of the fallen and innately evil condition of man, the God-as-spirit theology evolved through a series of early Christian controversies, most notably the Arian and Athanasian conflicts leading to the Council of Nicea in A.D. 325. With God pretty much established as a spirit, it remained only for the factions in Nicea to resolve the "separate God" concept of the Father, Son, and Holy Ghost, or continue being classified with pagans who had a multiplicity of gods. This was accomplished by declaring the Christian trinity "both visible and invisible" as well as separate and yet "of one essence." This "incomprehensible" and mysterious trinity satisfied most of the Church fathers and soon became accepted by most Christians in the Western World.

Departures from this traditional view were extremely rare and when a supposed departure took place, it could be questioned whether a departure really had been made at all. An example of this was the controversy that occurred in the early nineteenth century between the "orthodox" Christians and the Unitarians, whom the orthodox felt were moving away from such orthodox teachings as the three-in-one Trinity.

As the astute William Ellery Channing pointed out in an open letter published on the controversy in 1851, the controversy was perhaps more a question of semantics. He pointed out that everyone believed in the Father, the Son, and the Holy Spirit, both the Unitarians as well as the orthodox whom he called Trinitarians. Trying to point out how the two groups actually differed, however, he said, "The Trinitarian believes that the one God is three distinct persons, called Father, Son, and Holy Ghost; and he believes that each is the only true God, and yet that the three are only one God." The essence of Channing's observation, therefore, was that although religious groups may separate the Trinity into distinct terms, the three "distinct persons" still remain mysteriously "one," inseparable in power or divinity. Unitarians on the other hand, he pointed out, believe that only the Father possesses supreme Divinity (Ahlstrom, p. 395). So it was never really a case of any group at that time believing the Trinity

42

consisted of distinct personages. It was merely a question of where the supreme authority resided - in one God or in a three-in-one God. It was only when Joseph returned from the Sacred Grove that the anthropomorphic nature of God, new to nineteenth-century Americans, was revealed to a people who almost universally preferred the traditional mystery of an unrevealable spiritual Trinity. Such a preference is a natural consequence of observing the weaknesses and faults of one's fellow beings. It was just easier to accept a God who wasn't a physical being. Physical implies fallibility, and who wants to think of God in this way? To imagine a God so similar to ourselves was and still is a heretical departure from at least fifteen hundred years of preachings on the innately sinful and degrading nature of man.

Did Joseph Smith understand the heresy of this discovery? As Harold Bloom, Sterling Professor of Humanities at Yale University and a non-Mormon, objectively points out, "Anthropomorphism, or the idea that God could be human-all-too-human, is a poor notion anyway, as Joseph Smith implicitly understood" (Bloom, p.99). But Joseph had no options in revealing his radical discovery; he knew what he saw.

UNDEMOCRATICALLY CHOSEN LEADERS

Even before the advent of Jacksonian Democracy, American Protestants had prided themselves on the power of local congregations in choosing their spiritual leaders – and also in dismissing them when the occasion called for it. The author's own great great great grandfather was a member of a Dutch Reformed Church in Orange County, New York, at the time of the American Revolution. Because of the Tory sympathies of the minister, the Reverend John

43

M. Kern, the elders of the church democratically and dramatically chose to dismiss him. They met him at the door of the church one Sunday morning and handed him a walking cane and a pair of boots, symbolic of his dismissal.

Such congregational power was welcomed and enhanced even more with the coming of Jacksonian Democracy. No longer were professional religious leaders necessarily sent to preside over congregations without their consent. The period from the American Revolution to the rise of Mormonism was especially noted for the rise of popular religious leadership. Such preachers as Lorenzo Dow, Barton Stone, Alexander Campbell, William Miller, and Francis Asbury developed huge followings by the democratic technique of persuasive sermonizing. De Tocqueville, the French author of *Democracy in America*, summed it up when he remarked in amazement, "Where I expect to find a priest, I find a politician" (DeTocqueville, 1990, II, 306-7).

According to Mormon scholar Marvin Hill, the major objection of apostates from the Church in the late 1830s was "a concentration of authority at the top and authority's increasing control of every aspect of life" (Lannius & Hallwas, p.132). What the dissidents wanted was a more open society, more in line with the traditional democratic values and practices of American Protestantism. Democracy was the rage and byword, especially on the frontier. Joseph was well aware of these popular wants, but he resisted the popular approach to frontier religion.

The Lord seemed to offer little to compensate for the loss of such popular attractions as popular democracy. There was certainly no charming celebrity leadership as with modern televangelists when Joseph introduced these doctrines. Over time Joseph Smith developed the charisma of a popular religious leader, but

44

from the very beginning of the founding of the Latter-day Saint Church in 1830, adherents by the thousands flocked to his new banner without once hearing him preach, being convinced only by the messages of the missionaries. Joseph, like the leaders who would come after him, and those who filled the new leadership positions in his church, were chosen, he said, by the Lord. They would be popularly sustained many times over, but this was more of a formality and not to be confused with election. Democratically selected church leaders would have had far more appeal in Jacksonian America, but the Lord's Church was not to be a "democracy," no matter how much more acceptable that might have been.

"UNERRING" RELIGIOUS LEADER

Joseph Smith was not an unerring religious leader. He made it quite plain to his followers that he was a prophet only when he spoke as a Prophet. At other times he was fallible and admitted it. He even received and ordered published revelations that faulted him for his weaknesses (D&C 3:6, 5:21).

To his critics within and his enemies without, however, he was viewed as setting himself up as a religious dictator. It was at precisely this period of American history – the 1820s and 1830s – that anti-Catholic sentiment reached its apex among native Protestants. There was a deluge of anti-Catholic writings and even a pastoral letter by Episcopal bishops in 1829 warning of Papist perils. As the Catholic Church increased its American membership through an influx of immigrants, books and sermons against "Popery" became even more exaggerated and hysterical, culminating in such violent acts as the attack on and the burning of the Ursuline Convent in Massachusetts in 1834.

The focus of much of this anti-Catholic hostility was centered on the concept of a church that claimed an "infallible" leader – a tenet running directly contrary to Jacksonian egalitarianism, a principle achieved at great cost in the War for Independence from an "elitist" authoritarian government. This was why so much of the inflammatory anti-Catholic feeling was couched in such derogatory terms as "Popery" and "Popish."

Joseph Smith was well aware of the potential parallel that would be drawn between an "infallible" Pope, detested by so many Americans, and an "infallible" Prophet who also claimed direct communication with God. Although this scenario never developed in the anti-Mormon movement that took place, probably because of all the other more easily identifiable targets of criticism in Mormonism, it was a major probable hazard that a scheming charlatan would have avoided.

"POPISH" PRIESTHOOD

In carrying out a successful deceit, public perception is extremely important. Although many Protestant churches in the early nineteenth century had some of the same Priesthood offices as found in the newly restored Church of Jesus Christ, such as Elders, Teachers, and Deacons, the Lord revealed to Joseph Smith far more than religious offices.

There was to be a restoration of the ancient Priesthoods of Aaron and Melchizedek, with all the authority essential to perform ordinances in the Lord's name. Mormonism, like Catholicism, would emphasize the importance of apostolic authority and succession. Such authoritativeness, along with the Catholic-like offices of Priest and High Priest, would come strikingly close to the detested "Popish" Priesthood, at least in the perception of Jacksonian-era American Protestants.

Again, there is little evidence that the anti-Mormons made direct use of this parallel, but their failure to do so does not detract from the inherent risks of such thinking by potential converts to the Restored Church. Only the actual appearances of heavenly personages to restore the Priesthood could possibly have dissuaded Joseph from not instituting that important precept of the Gospel. Otherwise, it would have been a principle far too risky to implement in such a turbulent anti-"Popish" and anti-authoritarian era.

ADDITION TO BIBLE

The most apparent deviation the Saints made from traditional Protestantism was the addition of scripture – the *Book of Mormon*. As heretical as some of their other teachings might have been, it was nothing less than blasphemy to put another book on a par with the Bible. In a frontier agrarian society where citizens had little time for reading and even less money for acquiring the books to read, it was a matter of pride and a sign of traditional Christian faith to have at least a Bible on a cabin shelf, regardless of the cost. It did little good for the Latter-day Saints to remind their detractors that there was no Bible during the first three centuries of the Christian era. It did not faze their enemies to be reminded that their most beloved scripture, the King James version of the Bible, had already undergone a number of revisions with each change being, in essence, an addition or change in scripture. And it made no difference to opponents that John's warning about adding to "this book" (Rev.22:18) was a reference to the Book of Revelation since the Bible had not yet been compiled into a canon. Nor were the critics moved by a reminder that Moses had issued the same warning about adding to his words (Deut.4:2). Merely the claim of a book comparable to their cherished Scripture was blasphemous and deserved the harshest assault that could be brought to bear.

Such attacks and charges of heresy were not unexpected in a family such as the Smith's, whose New England ancestry was well grounded in the traditional Protestant devotion to the Book of Books. Joseph was also well aware that if merely developing a religious following was his objective, it was not only unnecessary to introduce new scripture, but it would be downright suicidal to the aims of any reformer who wished to remove the Bible from the pedestal as the only source of God's words. All of the reformers of the time period immediately preceding Joseph Smith, as well as the more traditional frontier theologians, continually debated such issues as election, grace, and baptism. But one of the doctrines they did not debate was the place of the Bible in their religions. This is demonstrated by an historic creedal agreement reached among reform and regular Baptists in Kentucky in 1801 that set a pattern for the beliefs of an increasingly large segment of the frontier religious community of the early nineteenth century. The first of their eleven creedal statements read, "We . . . do agree to unite on the following plan. 1st That the scriptures of the Old and New Testaments are the infallible word of God, and the only rule of faith and practice" (Ahlstrom, p. 441).

Just exactly what Joseph Smith was facing when he introduced his additional scripture to his fellow Americans can best be summed up by John W. Nevin, a nineteenth-century scholar of American Protestantism. After completing a study of fifty-three American sects of the 1840s, Nevin concluded that their single most unifying feature was the principle "No creed but the Bible" (Hatch, p. 81).

The Prophet Joseph didn't have to make a study of those sects. He also lived among them and understood full well what to expect by attempting to overthrow the one major principle upon which his potential Protestant converts and enemies alike agreed.

RIGID AUTHORIZED DOCTRINE

The Restored Gospel was not rigid in the sense that it could not change. After all, continuing revelation was a major tenet of the Lord's Church. It was rigid, however, in the sense that individual congregations had no sovereignty when it came to interpreting doctrine. Among the seething mass of Protestant denominations, however, independence of belief was esteemed almost an inalienable right of not only individual congregations but of the individuals within the congregations. The same John W. Nevin who noted the universality of the principle of "no creed but the Bible" among American Protestants, at the same time complained, in reference to the Bible, about that "book dropped from the skies for all sorts of men to use in their own way" (Hatch, p.182).

The rapid growth in the belief in private judgment on questions of religious doctrine grew out of the fulminations of frontier preachers. These popular leaders were the reformers preceding Joseph Smith who were lashing out at the strict doctrinal tenets being renewed after the Great Awakening. Now, ironically, these revisionists of American Protestantism were finding it increasingly difficult to retain the loyalty of their own followers whom they had helped imbue with the "private judgment syndrome."

Certainly the last kind of religion such proud adherents of private religious interpretation wanted was one that decreed unquestioning obedience to an authorized doctrine being established in the Restored Gospel. Both critics and

49

members of the Church of Jesus Christ of Latter-day Saints have privately and publicly questioned or marveled at the number of excommunications in the early history of the Restored Church. This becomes much easier to understand when recognizing the religious backgrounds of those early converts to Mormonism. The doctrinal discipline so essential in their new faith was simply too much of a culture shock for many of those steeped in the free-thinking frontier theology from which they had converted.

The Prophet's own family had themselves been part of this ecclesiastical liberation. To again fetter such free thinkers with precise and self-denying tenets would be the height of folly as Joseph well knew – unless the Lord was unmoved by American cultural restraints and freedoms.

A "FIRELESS" HELL

The God that holds you over the pit of hell, much as one holds a spider, or some loathsome insect over a fire, abhors you . . . he looks upon you as worthy of nothing else, but to be cast into the fire . . . It is nothing but his hand that holds you from falling into the fire every moment . . . There is no other reason to be given why you have not gone to hell, since you have sat here in the house of God, provoking his pure eyes by your sinful wicked manner of attending his solemn worship. Yea, there is nothing else that is to be given as a reason why you do not this very moment drop down into hell . . . a wide and bottomless pit, full of the fire of wrath. (Ferm, p.190)

These words from the famous sermon by Jonathan Edwards, "Sinners in the Hands of an Angry God," were preached by that famous New England Divine more than sixty years before the birth of Joseph Smith, but they describe perfectly hell as a place of eternal fiery torment, a concept held by the typical Protestant throughout American history. Congregations trembled when they heard their preachers describe the hell that was in store for all sinners. But that was the kind of eternal punishment they wanted to hear. It was what they were used to hearing and it was what their sinful neighbors and misbehaving children deserved. Any concept less than such a "Biblical" belief was heretical and could not be tolerated in a society intent on keeping the religious traditions of their forefathers. And the Prophet Joseph seemed to be breaking all their traditions when he described the nature of hell according to the Restored Gospel.

According to the Prophet Joseph, his critics learned, "A man is his own tormentor and his own condemner. Hence the saying, They shall go into the lake that burns with fire and brimstone. The torment of disappointment in the mind of man is as exquisite as a lake burning with fire and brimstone" (Smith, Joseph Fielding, p. 357). And the Book of Mormon describes the "pain, and anguish, which is like an unquenchable fire" in the breast of an unrepentant man (Mosiah 2:38). Thus, hell was a state of mind as well as an actual place, and that actual place was not a literal place of eternal punishment. It was, according to the Book of Mormon, a part of the world of spirits, a place of darkness and sorrow for the souls of the wicked "until the time of their resurrection" (Alma, 40: 14) and thus a place from which one could be redeemed.

Such a doctrine as this would have been one of the easiest to leave out of his theology, if it had been Joseph's theology. It would have had little bearing on the general theme of a Restored Gospel and would certainly have made his Church a little more acceptable to his neighbors. But it was the Lord's Church and however heretical such teachings were to potential converts to the Church, and probably even to Joseph himself, he knew they were part of the Restored Gospel and could not be left out regardless of the derision they would spawn.

NECESSITY OF GOOD WORKS

There is a certain irony that the well-known Protestant Work Ethic should have arisen among the very people who also were adherents to such doctrines as predestination. The Prophet Joseph and the early church leaders perceived predestination as a doctrine dangerously close to salvation by grace alone, a traditional Protestant tenet that was quickly modified in the Restored Gospel. Only a year after the Church was organized, Joseph received a revelation dealing with the subject that had been debated for so many years among American Protestants – the importance of good works versus salvation by grace alone: "Verily I say, men should be anxiously engaged in a good cause, and do many things of their own free will, and bring to pass much righteousness; For the power is in them, wherein they are agents unto themselves. And inasmuch as men do good they shall in no-wise lose their reward" (D&C 58:27-28).

It was not a case, as the Lord revealed, of accepting either Paul's admonition that "a man is justified by faith without the deeds of the law" (Rom. 3:28) or James's statement that "faith without works is dead" (James 2:20). It was a case of both faith and good works being as important as the two blades of a pair of scissors, an analogy used by C. S. Lewis. Such an analogy could not be seen, however, by Joseph's countrymen who again saw a cherished traditional belief crushed under foot by this new gospel.

The popularity of the frontier revivals in early nineteenth-century America

52

demonstrates perfectly the attachment the hard-living, hard-drinking, back-sliding, but good-intentioned frontier Americans had to the tenet of Salvation by Grace. Accounts of those revivals mention again and again the cases of back-sliders continually returning to be "saved," or of the seamy activities taking place at night meetings on the revival grounds. Some modern Protestant theologians refer to this as "cheap grace," which offers "salvation" without a sense of personal responsibility (*Encyclopedia of Mormonism*, 2:561).

Nevertheless, this was the type of salvation that appealed to so many early nineteenth-century Americans. The restored doctrine of placing an equal emphasis on the necessity of good works was not a doctrine that would necessarily arouse charges of blasphemy as much as such Latter-day concepts as additional scripture and an anthropomorphic God, but it was a doctrine that a great many Americans would certainly not find appealing. And the future of the Restored Gospel depended on its appeal. But the Lord knew, if Joseph perhaps didn't, that there is no better weapon in the battle for men's souls than the truth.

PROHIBITION OF TOBACCO AND LIQUOR

It was on February 27, 1833, when the Prophet Joseph received the revelation warning against the use of tobacco, wine, strong drinks, hot drinks, and urging greater use of healthy foods such as herbs, fruits, and grains. Strong drinks were interpreted and explained by Joseph to mean liquor, while hot drinks were coffee and tea. At this time in the United States, the use of tobacco, liquor, tea, and coffee were extremely widespread. It seems that almost without exception, foreigners who visited and wrote about their travels in this new nation were appalled and disgusted by the habit of almost all American men in their use of

53

tobacco and spitting in public. Writers such as Frances Trollope, Harriet Martineau, Captain Marryat, and even Charles Dickens, although finding much to admire in American society, were quite unanimous in their condemnation of that "filthy American habit." Charles Dickens complained that American men spit in the theaters, in Congress, and even at their dinner tables. He said that even in the courts "the judge has his spittoon, the crier his, the witness his, and the prisoner his" (Berger, p. 64). Such visitors even commented on the impossibility of eradicating this deeply ingrained habit.

Another widespread habit, visitors noted, was the propensity of Americans to consume vast quantities of liquor. Although few visitors complained about the quality of American liquor (in fact some even included recipes for their favorites in their writings), they were nevertheless astounded by the universal prevalence of "strong drinks," where drinking was everywhere common upon meeting, parting, and closing a bargain. Captain Frederick Marryat, an English author who visited American in 1837, described the closing of a property bargain between two Yankee farmers. Upon an agreement on price, one of the parties finalized it with "It's a bargain then (rising up), come let's liquor on it" (Marryat, p. 149).

Such habits were no different among the Latter-day Saints when Joseph announced his revelation in 1833. The Prophet had been prompted to go to the Lord in prayer because of the situation in the School of the Prophets held upstairs in the Whitney store in Kirtland in which Joseph and his family were living in 1833. Brigham Young described the circumstances: "Often when the Prophet entered the room to give the school instructions he would find himself in a cloud of tobacco smoke. This, and the complaints of his wife at having to clean so filthy a floor, made the Prophet think upon the matter, and he inquired of the Lord."

54

(Young, JD 12:158).

If the revelation Joseph received was nothing more than his method of solving the problem he encountered in the School of the Prophets, his "revelation" would have pertained only to the use of tobacco. Why would he have included liquor, tea, and coffee, which were certainly not problems to the Prophet or the members at that time? And certainly there would have been no reason to suggest more healthy foods since there is no evidence of either the knowledge of or need for such a dietary suggestion among the Latter-day Saints at that time. And certainly such a change in their customary drinking habits would not be welcomed by either members or potential members alike.

Historically speaking, it is true that it was several years before the Word of Wisdom actually became a commandment and before violators would receive the condemnation they do today. Nevertheless, the Lord, and apparently Joseph, took the revelation seriously and numerous attempts were made to enforce it. In 1834 Church officials in Kirtland discussed whether violators of the Word of Wisdom were qualified to hold Church positions. When asked his opinion, the Prophet declared, "No official member in this Church is worthy to hold an office, after having the Word of Wisdom properly taught him, and he, the official member neglecting to comply with, or obey" it (Backman,1983, p. 259). And at a meeting of the various quorums in Far West in May 1837, it was "Resolved unanimously that we will not fellowship any ordained member who will or does not observe the Word of Wisdom according to its literal reading" (Cannon & Cook, *Far West Record,* pp. 106-7). It is of interest to note that of the various charges brought up at Far West in 1838 against David Whitmer, one of the Three Witnesses, was his "wrong-doing in persisting in the use of tea, coffee, and tobacco" (HC, III, 4).

It doesn't take a psychological study of fraudulent behavior to understand that to enlist persons in a counterfeit scheme, one must offer the potential members whatever gives them pleasure – not deprive them of the comforts and gratifications they are used to. It's true that there are some individuals who are attracted to any group that requires forms of self-deprivation, but such persons do not form the potential market for converts that a highly successful organization must be able to tap. And certainly the Prophet Joseph, as shrewd as even his enemies called him, would not logically set up such a stumbling block as the Word of Wisdom to discourage conversion if the Restored Church was his own invention.

It is recognized that reform movements in alcoholic consumption and improved diets were underway at this period of history, but they had certainly not been successful in recruiting the masses, as is attested by the numerous foreign visitors who described American customs of the period. So it would have been foolhardy to add one more unpopular doctrine to the long list of radical and unpopular doctrines already revealed in the Restored Gospel. The only rational reason for it being done is that such a revelation – so incompatible to American culture at the time but proven so beneficial a century and a half later – must have originated with the Lord.

SACRIFICE OF TIME TO SERVE MISSIONS

In the 1830s the United States was an agrarian society with the vast majority of families living off the land. This was especially true on the frontier where the Saints were congregated. It was not until 1855 that the national census started to list occupations, so it is difficult to determine precisely the exact

56

percentage of Americans who were farmers when the Church was organized. The 1855 census for Cattaraugus County, New York, where the organization took place, however, lists 75 percent of adult males as farmers. Twenty-five years earlier, when the Founders met in the Whitmer cabin, the percentage would have been even higher.

Such a lifestyle, if the husband and father hoped to be successful in obtaining a subsistence for a family, meant almost ceaseless toil in tilling the soil, planting, cultivating and harvesting crops, caring for livestock 365 days a year, building fences, repairing buildings, and so forth. Among any frontier people, taking even one day per week off to attend church was a sacrifice that many husbands and fathers felt was simply too much to ask for.

And now with the advent of the Restored Gospel, we had a faith that asked those frontier farmers to sacrifice not only a few hours to attend Sabbath Day meetings, but to surrender entire years of their lives to serve extended missions. These were not young men, unmarried and with few responsibilities as they are today, but men with families and farms or businesses, who were asked to place their reliance entirely on the Lord and on already over-worked wives and children.

One example will illustrate a fairly typical missionary calling, of which there had been almost eighteen hundred by the time of Joseph's death in 1844 (*Church Almanac*, 1991-92, p. 335). Louisa Pratt's husband was sent from Nauvoo to serve a three-year mission in Tahiti, leaving Louisa and four young children behind. Louisa describes her husband's leaving: "The parting scene came. The two eldest daughters wept very sorely. We walked with them to the steamboat landing: he carried the youngest child in his arms . . . It was unfortunate at the last as he stept on to the steamboat the children saw him take his handkerchief from his eyes, they knew he was wiping away his tears (Godfrey, et al., pp. 13-14).

Neither were these departing men being asked to travel such long distances with assurances of travel and living expenses taken care of by savings accounts or their home congregations. They usually left on extended, often overseas assignments, without purse or script, going many times without food or shelter. Unlike the young missionaries the Church sends out today, many of these family men were called to serve numerous missions and there were cases of them receiving no more than a few hours warning. Such sacrifices would require a total commitment to a cause that becomes difficult for even devout members today to understand.

Such sacrifices also prompt a question, not of the reasons for such commitment, but the reasons for such a requirement in the first place. Many other successful faiths had prospered with a few voluntary missionaries or none at all. The question that must be answered is why so many were called to sacrifice so much amid such destitution and persecution as was prevalent in those early years. It was not that potential converts were unaware of the sacrifices they would also be required to make. They were well aware of the lives ahead of them by merely being acquainted with the missionaries who had been sent among them – men like themselves who had families and farms back home, demanding time and attention. Questions of whether they, as converts, would be capable of such sacrifice seemed to fade as they observed the faith of those missionaries – faith that their families would be cared for and blessed for the sacrifices of their husbands and fathers. Recognizing such faith as a desire of the Lord, not Joseph, left no room for further questions.

NATIVE AMERICANS AS SPIRITUAL BROTHERS

"All that is good and great in man, results from education; an uncivilized Indian is but a little way from a beast who, when incensed, can only tear and devour, but the savage applies the ingenuity of man to torture, and inflict anguish" (Loudon 1971, Preface v). Such was the general opinion held by most Americans about the native Americans in the early nineteenth century and expressed in a book about "Outrages committed by the Indians" published in Pennsylvania in 1808.

Public opinion had changed little when John Frost published his *Indian Wars of the United States* in 1856. In his preface he described Indian-White relations as "for the most part, a history of bloody wars, in which the border settlers have suffered all the horrors of Savage aggression "(Frost, p. 5).

It was into this anti-Indian climate of public attitude that the *Book of Mormon* was published, "Written to the Lamanites" as recorded on its title page. In March of that same year, 1830, it was revealed to Joseph the purpose of the Book of Mormon, "which is my word to the Gentile, that soon it may go to the Jew, of whom the Lamanites are a remnant" (D&C 19:27).

As if it were not enough to add additional scripture to their beloved Bible, it was even more blasphemous to most Americans, especially those on the frontier, to practically dedicate that new scripture to the salvation of those bloody savages who were holding up the progress of the white man's superior civilization. Joseph had no naive concepts of the Indians as many Europeans and New England intellectuals did. He realized the threats they posed to the white frontiersmen who felt the latter needed the land, but still he felt compelled to profess brotherhood to them. In a letter to W. W. Phelps in Missouri, Joseph wrote "between us and you the Indians are a spreading death and devestation wherever they go" (Jessee, p. 248).

Only someone abysmally ignorant or hopelessly defeatist would, on his own initiative, pursue such an unpopular course so prejudicial to his primary objective of attracting recruits. Seemingly not satisfied with the enemies he was making with his revelations and dedicated scripture, within months of the *Book of Mormon* publication, Joseph sent off the Church's first missionaries to preach to the Indians. Starting out in October 1830, this Lamanite Mission, which included such early Church stalwarts as Oliver Cowdery, Peter Whitmer, and Parley P. Pratt, traveled fifteen hundred miles on foot from New York to the Indian Country west of Independence, Missouri. Although of limited success among the Indians, it marked the beginning of the Church's long practice of taking the Gospel to Native Americans.

In spite of a lack of permanent success among the various tribes the Mormon missionaries initially encountered, the message did not change. Such continued consistency is evidence that Joseph did not emphasize the role of the Native Americans in the Restored Gospel to soften them up as potential converts. He had nothing, not even the hope of converting large numbers of natives, to gain from calling them "brothers." He continued to teach that the Lamanites were a chosen people who would eventually be brought back into the fold and enjoy all the blessings of the Restored Gospel. Such beliefs and teachings were not lost on the enemies of the Church, especially when the Saints set out to establish their Zion in Missouri, on the border of the "Indian Country." In 1836 at a mass meeting of anti-Mormons, a document was drawn up citing the reasons the Mormons must remove themselves from Clay County. A very effective accusation was that the Saints were holding communication with the Indians for the purpose of dispossessing the people of Western Missouri of their homes. The charge read: "In addition to all this, they are charged, as they have hitherto been, with keeping up a constant communication with our Indian tribes on the frontiers; in declaring even from the pulpit, that the Indians are a part of God's chosen people, and are destined by heaven to inherit this land, in common with themselves" (HC, III, 30).

Joseph's personal views on Native Americans, however, transcended the theological aspect of them as God's Chosen people, and perhaps made it a little less onerous to promulgate that view to his hostile frontier neighbors. His most personal feelings about the Indians were revealed in a journal entry in January 1842, when he wrote, "In the evening debated with John C. Bennett and others to show that the Indians have greater cause to complain of the(ir) treatment (by) the whites, than the Negroes" (HC 4:501).

In spite of how politically correct and socially acceptable the Latter-day Saint's position on Native Americans would be a century and a half later, it was totally unthinkable and even profane to consider the Indians as equals among the "brotherhood of man" in early nineteenth-century America. Joseph was certainly not unaware of such an attitude among his fellow Americans and he had obviously not abandoned hope of making converts among his frontier neighbors, who resented strongly the LDS doctrine of Indian equality. The factor Joseph was not free to ignore was that the Lord was using him as an instrument in declaring and emphasizing the spiritual equality and kinship of the Native Americans to the white race. It had been no coincidence, perhaps, that in the same year Congress passed the Indian Removal Act, uprooting thousands of Indians from their ancestral homes in Eastern United States, the Lord restored His Church to become the means of bringing the Lamanites back to their eternal home with the Lord.

PLURAL MARRIAGE

There would be no doctrine introduced by Joseph Smith that would generate more opposition and hostility than his revelation on plural marriage. The Prophet was well aware of the negative impact such a revelation could have on the Restored Church, which is the reason he hesitated so long to make it known or to attempt to practice the doctrine himself.

Evidence indicates it was made known as early as 1832 and possibly even much earlier. Elder Charles Walker refers in his journal to a sermon by Brigham Young, who said that while Joseph and Oliver Cowdery were translating the *Book of Mormon,* they had a revelation on plural marriage. Oliver, according to Brigham, wished to enter the order of plural marriage at once but was warned against it by Joseph who apparently was afraid of the consequences of such a radical doctrine. Oliver ignored Joseph's counsel and took a Miss Annie Lyman as a plural wife and, according to Brigham Young, from that time went into darkness and lost the spirit (*The Most Holy Principle,* 1970, 1:1-2).

In a discourse delivered in 1878, Joseph F. Smith stated,

> I here declare that the principle of plural marriage was not first revealed on the 12th day of July, 1843. It was written for the first time on that date, but it had been revealed to the Prophet many years before that, perhaps as early as 1832. About that time, or

subsequently, Joseph, the Prophet, entrusted this fact to Oliver
Cowdery; he [Cowdery] abused the confidence imposed in him,
and brought reproach upon himself, and thereby upon the church.
(JD 10:29)

It was undoubtedly as a result of the experience with his trusted associate
Oliver, and because of his own rational misgivings about the consequences of
such a doctrine, that Joseph waited another ten long years until Nauvoo was
settled before he revealed the doctrine more openly among his associates. He
probably received more revelations from the Lord in Kirtland and may himself
have taken a plural wife as early as 1835 (Backman,1983, p. 326). There seems
little question that some members had entered the practice without authorization
in Kirtland, justifying their actions by claiming that Joseph had taken a plural
wife. Still, the Prophet was extremely reluctant to make public such a sacred but
controversial tenet.

Because of its sacredness, Joseph believed such a holy and important
principle could not be revealed to the wicked and for this reason often denied its
practice to the general public. He feared, from his experiences with Oliver and
others in Kirtland, that many would use such information to justify their own
adulterous lives. It was a dilemma and one he would not voluntarily have selected
himself. It should seem rather obvious that the circumstances of Joseph's own
private life would dispel the charge by critics that the doctrine was "revealed" to
satisfy Joseph's own lustful desires. First of all, because of a life so full of
persecutions, the care of his own family, and his tireless work for the Church, he
simply lacked the time. His obvious love for Emma and her opposition to the
doctrine would discourage Joseph from doing much more than the formal

63

necessities of being sealed to other wives. And last and perhaps most telling, where are the children from his other marriages? His own large family with Emma would certainly indicate his ability to father children. Only a child of Sylvia Sessions Lyon has ever been claimed by one of Joseph's plural wives to be his offspring. This seems strange indeed since such descendents would be sure to hold esteemed positions among fellow members in the Church.

It was without a doubt that the doctrine of plural marriage, more than any other, ultimately brought about the apostasy of leading members in Nauvoo, the printing and destruction of the Expositor newspaper, and the martyrdom of Joseph and Hyrum. If the doctrine had not come from the Lord, not only could Joseph have not revealed the doctrine, one he was obviously reluctant to announce, but he could have "received" a new revelation halting the practice when it began to create "out-of-control" circumstances in Nauvoo. This was something, however, that he knew was up to the Lord. One of Joseph's plural wives, Eliza R. Snow, years after the Prophet's death, most succinctly stated the Prophet's position: "It may be asked, Why defend plurality of wives, since the United States government forbids its practice? The action of the executors of the government can neither change nor annihilate a fundamental truth; . . .the controversy is with God – not us" (*A Most Holy Principle*, 1970, 1:15-16).

CHAPTER VII

WOULD HAVE DISCOURAGED LEARNING

A man is saved no faster than he gets
knowledge, for if he does not get knowledge,
he will be brought into captivity.
- Joseph Smith

It is an axiom in the land of chicanery to keep the devotees uninformed. Following such an axiom, if chicanery had been involved in the restoration of the Christian Church by Joseph Smith, he would not only have targeted for conversion the ignorant and easily deluded, but would have made every attempt to keep the new followers unlearned once they were in the Church. If pretense and deceit is the foundation upon which an organization is established, the light of education and knowledge is the last thing to which a charlatan would want his recruits exposed. Some of the Prophet's most basic teachings are evidence of his desire for his followers to be knowledgeable. Salvation, he taught, depended upon rising above all of one's enemies, not the least of which was ignorance. In an epistle to his people from the Liberty Jail in March of 1839, he wrote "But I beg leave to say unto you, Brethren, that ignorance, superstition and bigotry placing itself where it ought not, is oftentimes in the way of the prosperity of this Church" (Smith, *Teachings*, p. 138).

Actually, in the case of Joseph Smith and the restoration of the Church of Jesus Christ, the Prophet transgressed in two significant ways a "pretender's" axiom of keeping followers ignorant. First, he made his appeal to and attracted some of the most learned and intelligent religious seekers of the early nineteenth century. Second, from its very inception, Joseph emphasized both secular and religious education through the establishment of schools and even a university.

65

Let us look first at the type of people attracted to Mormonism during its early years.

In his book *The Uncommercial Traveler*, Charles Dickens described visiting an LDS emigrant ship about to depart from England in 1863. Upon boarding the ship Mr. Dickens noted three particular characteristics of the Saints about to depart for the New World. He noted first the large number sitting about writing letters to friends and relatives left behind, indicating a higher than normal educational level for emigrants. This characteristic, plus the other two characteristics, their cheerfulness and their apparent shipboard organization, led Mr. Dickens to refer to these Latter-day Saint emigres as "strikingly different from all other people in like circumstances" and "the pick and flower of England" (Mulder, pp. 334-37).

Another English author, Samuel M. Smucker, wrote one of the more objective histories of the Mormons in the nineteenth century. In his book *The Religious, Social, and Political History of the Mormons,* published in 1881, Smucker describes some earlier research about Mormon emigration from Great Britain:

> During the year 1850, the Mormon emigration amounted to nearly two thousand five hundred. Being desirous to know something of the class of persons who emigrated under Mormon auspices . . . the writer made inquiries at the office in Liverpool of Messrs. Pilkington and Wilson, the shipping-agents for the New Orleans packets. The principal manager of this branch of their business, who is thus thrown into frequent intercourse with the Mormons furnished the following statement – "With regard to

Mormon Emigration, and the class of persons of which it is

composed, they are principally farmers and mechanics, with some

few clerks, surgeons, & c. They are generally intelligent and well

behaved, and many of them are highly respectable." (Smucker,

1881, p. 298)

Admittedly, these reports were made several years after the Prophet

Joseph's death, but the doctrines attracting such people were the same as those

that appealed to the similarly select "seekers" twenty or thirty years earlier. And

the sentiments of objective witnesses in that period of time were comparable to

Charles Dickens' observations.

John Corrill, a convert who eventually turned against the Church and its

leadership at Far West, Missouri, had visited Kirtland, Ohio, in 1835 before his

excommunication and described the Latter-day Saints he encountered there as

inspired "with an extravagant thirst after knowledge" (Givens, p. 238).

Even those actively opposed to the Church often recognized and admitted

to a fact other anti-Mormons, for obvious reasons, denied in regard to the

intellectual characteristics of the Saints. John H. Eells, an anti-Mormon from

Elyria, Ohio, visited Kirtland in 1836, and in a letter to a Mr. Leavill, written on

April first of that year, described the Mormons he met there as deluded. He

nevertheless characterized them as

"very eager to acquire education. Men, women and children lately

attended school [reference to the School of the Prophets], and they

are now employing Mr. [Joshua] Seixas, the Hebrew teacher, to

instruct them in Hebrew; and about seventy men in middle life,

from twenty to forty years of age, are most eagerly engaged in study. They pursue their studies alone until twelve o'clock at night, and attend to nothing else. Of course many make rapid progress. I notice some fine looking and intelligent men among them . . . They are by no means, as a class, men of weak minds." (Mulder, 1973, 88)

Thomas F. O'Dea, a non-Mormon Professor of Sociology at the University of Utah, wrote in 1957, "If the Restored Church did not pull from the already educated classes, which they often did, they at least appealed to the more sophisticated or intelligent – those who would then be more prone to encourage and demand greater formal education." O'Dea went on to point out that Mormonism neither is nor was a "proletarian movement." The movement began, he noted, in a part of the state of New York with the highest proportion of cosmopolitan Yankee residents and with one of the highest proportions of children enrolled in school (O'Dea, p.10).

Another authority speaking on the same subject was Rodney Stark, Professor of Sociology and Comparative Religions at the University of Washington. In his book, *The Rise of Christianity*, published in 1996, he noted that "Those who first accepted Joseph Smith's teachings were better educated than their neighbors and displayed considerable intellectualism" (Stark, p.39).

This appears to be the case when we look specifically at some of the earliest converts to the Church. We here find an amazing number of well-educated or at least highly intelligent individuals. This is of significant interest when we consider how little formal education the Prophet Joseph had and yet seemed eager and able to surround himself with associates of much greater learning. A typical entry in Joseph's diary is found for November 2, 1835, which

records him traveling with Sidney Rigdon, Oliver Cowdery, and Frederick G.
Williams to Willoughby College to hear Dr. Piexotte lecture on physics
(Conkling, p.78). Surrounding himself with friends with such a thirst for
knowledge would be an extremely risky procedure if Joseph had anything that
needed to be kept hidden. Consider the following associates.

Set apart as a counselor in the First Presidency where he served from 1833
to 1844, was Sidney Rigdon, one of the Church's greatest orators of that time.
Until his conversion in 1830, he had been an extremely popular Baptist minister
and later a Campbellite minister in Ohio. When Joseph Smith was nominated for
President of the United States in 1844, Sidney received the Vice-presidential
nomination.

Oliver Cowdery, one of the three witnesses, was a school teacher when he
first met Joseph Smith. After his excommunication in 1838 and until he rejoined
the Church ten years later at Council Bluffs, he practiced law in Michigan.

In February of 1835 the members of the First Quorum of the Twelve were
selected in Kirtland. Members of that first group of twelve leaders were unusual
in frontier America for their leadership and intellectual accomplishments.

Lyman Johnson, one of those twelve, was excommunicated three years
after his appointment but remained friendly to his former associates and practiced
law until his death in 1856. Orson Hyde was proficient in several branches of
education, became founder and publisher of a newspaper in Kanesville (now
Council Bluffs), and later became an active member of the Territorial legislature
in Utah. Parley P. Pratt, founder and editor of the Millennial Star in Great Britain,
helped form a constitution for the Provisional Government of Deseret (Utah
Territory) and was elected to the Senate in the Territorial legislature. Orson Pratt,

who was several times speaker of the House of the Territorial legislature, had lectured a number of times on astronomy and math to large audiences in Scotland and England. He authored several books and left, at the time of his death, a manuscript on differential calculus, containing original principles. John Boynton, who was excommunicated but remained friendly to the Church throughout his life, lectured on natural history, geology, and other sciences. By 1886 he had his name listed on thirty-six inventions in the Patent Office, including weapons used during the Civil War.

And so it went. These were men too honest, as many of their non-Mormon associates testified at one time or another, to be fraudulent themselves and too astute to be victimized by a pretender. But in addition to attracting individuals of this caliber to the Restored Church, Joseph set out to produce educated leaders within the Church.

Only three years after the Church was organized, Joseph established the School of the Prophets in an upstairs room at the Newel K. Whitney store in Kirtland. This might very well have been the first adult education program in America. Actually, Church members were told a few years later by their leaders that one of the principle reasons for gathering to Kirtland was to provide members with educational advantages. "Education can only be obtained", they were told, "by living in a compact society; so compact, that schools of all kinds can be supported" (Backman, *The Heavens Resound,* p.263). So, beginning in 1833, instruction began and continued through four winter seasons. Topics were not limited to doctrine but secular subjects were discussed and taught as well. The Lord told Joseph that the purpose of the school was for "instruction in all things" (D&C 88:127). "Teach ye diligently . . . that ye may be prepared in all things . . .

70

Seek learning, even by study and also by faith" (D&C 88:77-79, 118). Brigham Young, in the *Journal of Discourses*, tells us that "the brethren came to that place for hundreds of miles to attend school in a little room probably no larger than eleven by fourteen" (JD, 12:158).

When the room was outgrown, the school was moved into the new printing office and later into the newly finished Temple, where penmanship, arithmetic, grammar, and geography were presented along with doctrinal subjects. Heber Kimball noted that 400 attended the school in the winter of 1835. "The Elders and church," he noted in his journal, "had been previously commanded to seek learning and study the best books, and get a knowledge of countries, kingdoms, languages &c., which inspired us with an untiring thirst after knowledge" (Jessee, p.651). By the winter of 1836-37, in spite of persecution and internal conflicts, as many as 150 men were still attending sessions in the Temple school rooms.

Meanwhile, a similar school, called the School of the Elders, had been set up in Missouri. It began in 1833 with Parley P. Pratt as teacher (Barrett, p. 235). In the very first issue of the *Evening and Morning Star*, a Church publication edited by W. W. Phelps in Independence beginning in June, 1832, the Lord, through the Prophet Joseph, urged that "The disciples should lose no time in preparing schools for their children, that they may be taught as is pleasing unto the Lord, and brought up in the way of holiness. Those appointed to select and prepare books for the use of school, will attend to that subject as soon as more weighty matters are finished."

Although Jackson County had been settled several years before the Saints arrived in 1831 and even had a Court House by that time, there were no means of educating the children in that area. Thus it was that the first schools in Jackson County were established by the Mormons (Bennion, pp. 17-18).

In 1836, after being expelled from Jackson and later Clay Counties, the Saints began settlements farther north on Shoal Creek. The largest settlement became Far West, which by the spring of 1838 had more than 150 houses, many of them the homes of school teachers. These well-educated Saints not only staffed the school houses in Far West, which were among the first buildings erected, but several were hired by Missourians to teach their children. One Mormon school teacher, Eliza Maria Partridge, wrote in her journal: "It was no uncommon thing in those times for our Mormon girls to go out among the Missourians and teach their children for a small remuneration" (Barrett, p. 366).

After being forced from Missouri in the winter of 1838-39, the Saints gradually gathered at Commerce in Illinois in 1839. Renaming their city Nauvoo, the Saints again forged ahead with their own school system, this time under the supervision of the Board of Regents of the projected municipal University of Nauvoo. Utilizing a system of common (public) and subscription (private) schools, it has been estimated that some twelve hundred children were receiving formal schooling in Nauvoo only three years after its founding (Givens, p. 242).

Perhaps the epitome in his optimistic endeavors to provide education for his people was Joseph's decision to adopt John C. Bennett's recommendation for a university only two years after their expulsion as destitute refugees from Missouri. In February 1841 the University of the City of Nauvoo was created and its chancellor, board of regents, and registrar appointed. Professor Stark noted that "the Mormons established a municipal university at a time when higher education was nearly nonexistent in the United States" (Stark, p.40).

Although there was never enough time in Nauvoo's history to build a formal central campus, several public buildings were utilized for that purpose, including the Masonic Hall, the Seventies Hall, and the Red Brick Store on the Flats, and the Concert Hall and the Temple on the Hill..

Subjects such as trigonometry, surveying, navigation, differential and integral calculus, philosophy, astronomy, and chemistry were advertised and taught by a number of qualified professors like Orson Spencer, a graduate of Union College in New York; Sidney Rigdon, who taught Church History, rhetoric, and literature; the Pratt brothers and Gustavus Hills, who headed the Department of Music (Miller & Miller, pp. 89-90). Perhaps the best known and most competent professor was Orson Pratt who taught courses in the fields of science and math and was, as previously noted, a popular lecturer in the British Isles.

A visiting U. S. Army officer to Nauvoo noted in 1842 that because of the "learned footing" upon which the Saints were establishing their religion, "ecclesiastical history presents no parallel to this people" (Givens, p. 251).

It might well be asked why the Prophet would put so much emphasis on secular learning – that appeared so traditionally at odds with organized religion and would certainly be even more incongruous and absurd if Joseph had been the author of a complex fraud more likely discernible by educated and informed followers. The answer, of course, is that Joseph had no fear of exposure, because there was nothing to expose other than the knowledge that the Lord had revealed to him in the section 29 of the Doctrine and Covenants in 1830 that "all things to the Lord are spiritual" (D&C, 29:34) and thus all subjects were worthy of knowing.

Joseph's desires to see the Saints educated in secular as well as spiritual matters did not end with his death. In 1870, after only twenty-two years in Utah, the percentage of school attendance there was higher than in Pennsylvania, New York, or Massachusetts. Ten years later illiteracy among Utahans over the age of ten was 5 percent compared to a national average of 13 percent (*A Non-Mormon*, p.11). One hundred and fifty years later, the Church's educational system had extended to more than ninety countries and territories involving more than 420,000 students and utilizing more than 19,000 employees and teachers, the largest private educational system in the world (*Encyclopedia of Mormonism*, 2:444). This would indeed be a rather inconceivable testimony to the aspirations of a man whom critics claim built his church on the tenets of duplicity and ignorance.

CHAPTER VIII

WOULD HAVE AVOIDED EXHIBITING
ORIGINAL *BOOK OF MORMON* INSCRIPTIONS

"After his return he came to see me again, and told
me that, among others, he had consulted Professor
Anthon, who thought the characters in which the
book was written very remarkable, but he could
not decide exactly what language they belonged
to. Martin had now become a perfect believer."
Rev. John A. Clark, Palmyra

Few frauds could be easier to expose than the fabricating of an ancient

manuscript claimed to be written in an unknown tongue based on an existing

classical language and then approaching a recognized expert in classical

languages seeking confirmation of its authenticity. Numerous literary frauds have

been attempted throughout history and exposed without the impostor ever

attempting verification by submitting their fraud to be analyzed by an expert in

the relevant field.

One of the best-known literary impostors was Annius, a Dominican born

in Viterbo in 1432. Claiming to have dug up some ancient works of such authors

as Berosus, Manetho, Cato, and Fabius Pictor, Annius published seventeen works

of antiquities. Honored by such well-known persons as Pope Alexander Borgia,

by being made Master of the Palace, Annius steadfastly refused to reveal where

he found the manuscripts or what they even looked like. Obviously fraudulent, it's

possible Annius himself had been imposed upon, but since he refused to reveal

the source of his discovery, he is considered one of history's most notorious

frauds. In 1765 James MacPherson, a scholar of ancient languages, published the

Poems of Ossian (in rhythmic prose), a 400 page epic claimed to have been written by an ancient Gaelic bard. MacPherson was accused of being a fraud and challenged to produce the original manuscript. He promised to do so but never did, knowing it could undoubtedly be disproved by experts. Those works, however, are still quoted today and believed by thousands in spite of MacPherson's unwillingness to submit any proof. Joseph Smith, on the other hand, submitted samples of the writing from the plates and had witnesses – and still millions disbelieve him.

Another extraordinary impostor was Joseph Vella, a Sicilian, who in 1794 claimed to have come into possession of seventeen lost books of Levy printed in Arabic. Even before the publication of some of these works, Vella was loaded with honors and pensions. Eventually, when the original manuscripts were demanded, he took an entirely unrelated Arabic volume on Mohammed's life and, altering the text with dots, flourishes, and strokes, submitted it as one of his original finds. It was only long after the publication of the "translation" and acceptance by thousands throughout Europe that an Orientalist examined a facsimile and discovered it to be a history of Mohammed and his family.

Again, Joseph Smith not only detailed his source (as inconceivable as it must have appeared), but went so far as to make a transcription of some of the original writings and submit it to the most renowned experts available to him. Such submission was for the edification of Martin Harris and not himself. Martin, one of Joseph's first followers, was a born skeptic and desired verification from some "experts" in the field. That the submission to professionals was Martin's idea is found in one of the first writings of Joseph Smith dealing with the beginning of Mormonism. Written in 1832 and referring to the man who gave him fifty dollars to help him move to Harmony, Joseph wrote of Martin, "and (he)

76

immediately came to Su(s)quehanna and said the Lord had shown him that he must go to New York City with some of the c(h)aracters so we proceeded to coppy some of them and he took his Journey to the Eastern Cittys and to the Learned" (Jessee, p.7).

Submission to the professionals was also designed, of course, to fulfill the prophesy found in Isaiah 29:11 ("I cannot read a sealed book"). Otherwise, if the transcription had truly been fraudulent and these experts had denounced it as one later claimed, Joseph, believing that verification was essential, would never have attempted publication.

Were these experts so respected and recognized that they would have had an impact on Joseph's decision to publish the translation?

One of the first experts Martin Harris visited was Dr. Samuel L. Mitchill. He not only taught at Columbia but also was the organizer and vice president of Rutgers Medical College from 1826 to 1830. He was a member of several scientific and scholarly societies and author of several scholarly books and pamphlets. Contemporaries called him a "living encyclopedia" (BYU Studies, Spring, 1970, p. 334).

The most respected linguist Harris visited, however, was Charles Anthon, Professor of Classical Studies at Columbia College from 1820 to 1867. He was to author more than thirty books and according to the *Dictionary of American Biography,* his influence upon the study of classics in mid-nineteenth-century America was probably greater than any other man (DAB, 1:314).

Wanting verification for what he apparently had some reservations about, Harris therefore took the transcription to the most highly respected experts in the country, with Joseph showing no reluctance in permitting it.

But did Joseph need the verification of any fellow man? He undoubtedly would have welcomed it – and according to Martin Harris, he received it – but it was certainly not essential.

Although we are not told who initiated Harris's trip to New York, we do know that he was being buffeted by a disbelieving wife and he had a well-established reputation to consider. He had not been interested in investigating Joseph's claims until members of his family became interested, and it was his lack of faith that delayed his witnessing the angel and the plates when Oliver Cowdery and David Whitmer received their witness. It was apparently important to the Lord that Martin Harris deliver the transcription to Charles Anthon and receive the verification since, as it turned out, his support would be important for the publication of the Book of Mormon. Because he returned from his visit to Professor Anthon enthused to continue his work with the Prophet and later willing to mortgage his farm to pay for the publication of the Book of Mormon, it appears obvious he received the verification he wanted from Professor Anthon. It is extremely unlikely that Harris would fabricate his story since he was skeptical in the first place. The trip to New York was expensive, time consuming, and certainly unnecessary if Harris intended to accept Joseph's story of the plates regardless of what he learned there.

Joseph, on the other hand, had everything to lose by allowing Martin to take the transcription to New York unless he was confident of the outcome.

First of all, did he know at that time that the Book of Mormon could not be published without Martin's willingness to mortgage his farm? Martin had made the trip to see Anthon in February of 1828, well over a year before the manuscript was ready for publication. And when the time came, Joseph tried other avenues before falling back on the resources of Martin. Second, was substantiation by Professor Anthon the only thing that would convince Martin Harris to continue his support of the Prophet? Remember, Martin would soon be privileged to view the plates. Such a witnessing would be far more convincing to a skeptic like Martin than a letter from a college professor in New York. The Lord was aware of the future witnessing and Joseph could have asked for it any time he felt it was essential. Even though Joseph was not yet aware of the willingness of the Lord to give him the witnesses, he already had believers other than Martin, followers he risked losing if an "expert" declared his transcripts fraudulent.

The author J. N. Washburn, writing on this subject in 1954, pointed out that if Joseph "had the intelligence to write the least chapter in the Book of Mormon he must certainly have had enough to avoid doing the one thing most likely to destroy any hope he might have had of deceiving anyone ... . Certainly he would not have sent his fake inscriptions to a linguist" (Washburn, p. 153).

Modern writers, both LDS and anti-Mormon, quibble over Harris's account of his visit. They are missing the main point – which was Joseph's willingness to submit the writings to the most learned men of the time. It is not important whether Anthon and Mitchill verified the translation. (Actually, Anthon verified the transcription as being some type of Egyptian – verifying the translation would have been impossible to anyone without a background in reformed Egyptian.) What was important was that Joseph at that time knew practically nothing about classical languages but was willing to expose the transcription to the most prominent scholars of the day.

The only logical reason for the route pursued by Joseph, therefore, was an apparent total confidence in an expert's acceptance of the transcription as authentic and Joseph's knowledge that a prophesy had to be fulfilled.

How then do we explain Anthon's denial of his authentication? Martin Harris's testimony sounds credible since he returned from his visit to New York, anxious to continue helping Joseph in moving his work forward. How credible was Professor Anthon's later denial? Let's briefly investigate that, because therein lies the evidence of who was the most credible – Anthon or Harris? And more importantly, therein also is the answer as to the credibility of Joseph versus his critics.

For what actually happened between Martin Harris and Professor Anthon, we can rely only on the believability of their own statements and the fact, as previously pointed out, that Martin returned from New York ready to support Joseph in whatever he asked.

Martin Harris, in his report of the incident, which is well known to most Latter-day Saints, described showing the transcription from the plates along with their translation to the Professor. Anthon, he tells us, declared both the characters and the translation as correct in his estimation. Upon a request for his opinion in writing, Anthon obliged, but on his leaving, Martin was asked the source of the writings. When told they had been revealed to a young man by an angel, the Professor asked for the certificate back and tore it up, saying there was no such thing as ministering angels. When he asked to see the original plates, Dr. Anthon was told that part of them was sealed and Martin was forbidden to bring them. Anthon then said he could not read a sealed book, fulfilling the prophesy of Isaiah. Martin said he left the Professor's home and went to Dr. Mitchill of Rutgers Medical College who sanctioned what Anthon had said regarding the characters and their translation. Mr. Harris then returned home to wind up

80

important affairs in Palmyra and to devote his time to helping Joseph continue his work.

Six years later, as hostility increased against the Mormons, an anti-Mormon by the name of E. D. Howe wrote to Anthon requesting verification of what Martin Harris had claimed about his visit to New York. Anthon responded in a letter to Howe on February 17, 1834, saying that he had been asked but declined writing out any such authentication of the transcription and had told Harris he considered the whole thing a scheme to cheat the farmer out of his money. The entire letter is published in Smucker's *History of the Mormons* (pp. 37-39).

Seven years later, upon receiving another request concerning his connection with the Book of Mormon from Reverend Dr. T. W. Coit, Rector of Trinity church, Rochelle, West Chester County, New York, Professor Anthon answered in a letter dated April 3, 1841. In that letter, taken from *Gleanings by the Way* by Rev. John A. Clark, D. D., Anthon stated that no one, until Reverend Coit, had ever requested from him a statement in writing about the Harris incident – an obvious contradiction to his answer to the request received earlier from E. B. Howe. He then proceeded to tell the Reverend Coit that he did write out a certificate for Harris, denying the authenticity of the characters and translation, another contradiction to what he had told Mr. Howe about refusing to write his opinion of what Harris had shown him. Anthon's denial of what Harris reported can undoubtedly be ascribed to the desire of the learned Professor to remove himself as far as possible from appearing to support the detested Mormon sect in any way. His contradictions in the two letters were not necessary for that purpose, however, and can only be explained by his apparent lack of credibility as a reliable source of the truth.

After considering this lack of credibility on the part of Professor Anthon, however, it still appears that the most persuasive argument supporting Joseph's Prophetic calling does not rest on the veracity of either Anthon or Harris but on the decision of Joseph to submit the copy of the characters and their translation for study by such a respected linguist as Professor Charles Anthon. If fraudulent, there would have been everything to lose and nothing essential to be gained. With no fraud involved it is apparent that the trip to New York by Martin Harris was to serve three essential purposes. It was to fully convince Joseph's most doubting but important associate of the truthfulness of the work Joseph was doing; it was to fulfill Biblical prophesy; and it was to demonstrate to the world the credibility of Joseph Smith as a Prophet of the Lord.

CHAPTER IX

WOULD HAVE CREATED LESS REFUTABLE THEOLOGY

"Unafraid, Joseph Smith left for examination by
posterity an unparalleled array of documents. In
this he is distinguished and alone."
- Ariel L. Crowley

In the shadowy world of deception and fraud, the paramount thought in
the mind of the deceiver is the element of exposure and how to lower the risk
factor. There are some very obvious things Joseph should or should not have done
to have lowered the risk factors. His refusal to follow such a route should prompt
some question in the minds of his critics.

Why, for example, would Joseph invent a new archaeology involving
metal plates instead of putting the ancient manuscript on parchment as with the
case of the fictitious but more authentic sounding Spaulding manuscript? Why
would Joseph have devised an unknown ancient language instead of putting the
writing in easily researched and more acceptable ancient Hebrew?

Obviously, the greater the number of fraudulent details in the ruse, the
greater will be the risk of exposure also. The safest route to success therefore,
would be to limit the number of details, especially if such particulars involve an
unknown past culture that can easily be made known by future discoveries. And
certainly a charlatan would not offer details of a remote and obscure geographic
world region that would certainly be explored in some future time, thus exposing
the entire imposture. Universally accepted scientific and theological laws would
not be tampered with if credibility is to be maintained to any degree. If any part
of the fraud is to be displayed to experts and scholars by way of publication, the
writings must be scrupulously researched and composed and painstakingly edited

to remove any contradictions, inconsistencies, anachronisms, and literary and historical inaccuracies. If the publication is to be passed off as an ancient document, the risk is even greater and must be either composed or edited by an expert in the language and culture of the people represented in the document. The safest route to success by any impostor, therefore, would be to never counterfeit anything more complex than modest sized letters or documents. A book of any size, especially a 500 - page historic epic, would be a totally unacceptable risk. No such unique religious/historic epic as the Book of Mormon had ever been successfully entrusted to the world's belief in such a precipitous manner and Joseph Smith was well aware of that fact.

Finally, if a charlatan expects long-term success, he would not make specific prophecies of events to occur easily within his lifetime or that of his followers. One cannot escape the future and the proof of such prophecies. Modern-day prophets come and are soon disproved by the passage of time, with the exception of Joseph Smith and, some might add, Nostradamus. In the latter case, however, the prophecies are worded in such an ambiguous and obscure manner, it is possible to claim success for almost any of them. Joseph, however, was never ambiguous; his prophecies and teachings were direct, easily understood, and left no doubt he expected their fulfillment and acceptance.

The most exacting proof in determining the legitimacy of a prophet is to test his revelations and teachings. If, over a period of time, enough of what the Lord had revealed to him actually comes to pass or is proven to be true, there is reason to consider the validity of that person's claim to being a prophet. So it is with Joseph Smith. There is even more reason to accept Joseph as a prophet today than there was fifty years ago, just as there was more reason to accept him then

84

than there was one hundred years earlier. As time passes, more and more evidence accumulates supporting the Book of Mormon and the teachings of Joseph Smith. The most dramatic way to demonstrate the truth of this thesis is to simply enumerate and explain, where necessary, a sampling of the facts associated with the Book of Mormon and the teachings of the Prophet that have been sustained by science and scholarship over the past 170 years. For greater detail or more examples, refer to any of the sources listed in this chapter.

MULEK

One of the characters in the *Book of Mormon* is Mulek, son of Zedekiah who established one of the *Book of Mormon* peoples in the New World after escaping the sack of Jerusalem in 587 B. C. Until recently, Biblical scholars believed all the sons of Zedekiah were killed (2 Kings 25:1-10) although the Bible does not say "all." Recently, Hebrew scholars have reported finding evidence of a surviving son of Zedekiah, whose name when shortened as often happened with Biblical names, would be Mulek. A prominent Near Eastern specialist, a non-Mormon, was asked to comment on this finding. His response was, "If Joseph Smith came up with that one, he did pretty good" (Welch, *Reexploring the Book of Mormon*, p. 144).

HORSES & CHARIOTS

Horses are mentioned several times in the *Book of Mormon*, a fact that has delighted LDS critics, who for generations have had scholars support their contention that horses did not exist in *Book of Mormon* times; they were brought to the New World by the Spaniards.

Now the possibility of horses being used by Nephites is no longer arbitrarily dismissed. Scientific reports ranging from the *Missouri Archaeologist* in 1941 to the *Journal of Mammalology* in 1957 to a Miami Museum of Science newsletter in 1978 all present evidence of the possibility of horses among the natives of Pre-Columbian America. Such disclosures have been extremely disconcerting to *Book of Mormon* critics, as was the discovery of wheeled toys in *Book of Mormon* sites, proving that the chariots mentioned in the books of Alma and 3 Nephi were not an impossibility after all (Welch, *Reexploring the Book of Mormon,* p. 100).

Even if horses did not exist in the Western Hemisphere before the coming of the Spaniards, that would not mean the Book of Mormon people did not train some kind of large animal to be ridden and gave it a name that Joseph Smith could only have translated as horse, since that was the animal he was most familiar with that men rode. We must remember that when the American bison was first encountered, the Europeans called them buffalo after an animal that was most familiar to them. The fact that there was never a "buffalo" on the Great Plains does not mean that no animal similar to it, namely the "bison," ever existed in the New World.

WORDPRINTS

Some of the most convincing evidence of the authenticity of the *Book of Mormon* has been made possible only with the advent of modern computers. A fairly new method of determining the authorship of anonymously written documents and letters is now possible using what is called "wordprints." Each author has his or her distinctive pattern of word usage, easily identified when subjected to computer analysis. For generations, the specific authorship of each of the *Federalist Papers*, written by Alexander Hamilton, James Madison, and John Jay to a New York newspaper encouraging the adoption of the new Constitution, has been a mystery since specific names were not attached to each of the letters. Using computer wordprints, and to the delight and satisfaction of American historians, experts have now identified which of the three men wrote each letter.

In 1980 the *Book of Mormon* was put to the test to see if the critics were right. Was this "sacred" scripture written by Joseph Smith or an associate or perhaps copied from another nineteenth-century author, as detractors charged? In that year three experts in statistics, Wayne Larsen, Alvin Rencher, and Tim Layton, ran a wordprint analysis on the *Book of Mormon*. The results of that trial were later verified in a Berkeley Group study published in 1987. Both groups concluded that the Book of Mormon was written originally by several authors and that none of the writings matched those of Joseph Smith, Sidney Rigdon, Solomon Spaulding, or any nineteenth-century writing style. The actual Berkeley Group report concludes:

> By using a new wordprint measuring methodology
> which has been verified, we show that it is statistically
> indefensible to propose Joseph Smith or Oliver Cowdery
> or Solomon Spaulding as the author of the 30,000 words
> from the Book of Mormon manuscript texts attributed
> to Nephi and Alma. Additionally these two Book of
> Mormon writers have wordprints unique to themselves. . .
> Therefore, the *Book of Mormon* measures multiauthored,
> with authorship consistent to its own internal claims.

(Griffith, pp. 83-84)

COSMIC URBAN SYMBOLISM

Much of the evidence supporting the authenticity of the *Book of Mormon* is subtle and complex and escapes the attention of members and critics alike. Such is the case with what is known as Cosmic Urban Symbolism – a concept of a capital city or ceremonial center symbolically representing the structure of a sacred universe. This abstraction visualized in city planning was common in Southeast Asia, the Mediterranean, Africa and in Central America south to Peru. The existence of such symbolism was unknown in Europe and the United States in 1830, yet it is pervasive throughout the *Book of Mormon* (Olsen, pp. 79-92).

And speaking of city planning, isn't it strange that if Joseph or another nineteenth-century author had created the *Book of Mormon* epic, they wouldn't have devised a more believable description of native cultures, including such authentic characteristics as teepees or wigwam villages, canoes and deerskin clothing, drums, tomahawks, and so forth? And yet there is none of this in the *Book of Mormon*. Instead, we find the creation of unfamiliar and architecturally complex cities, where readers appear to be offered the choice of accepting the hard-to-believe reality of an unknown civilization or a fraudulent fantasy. The easier, less refutable route to acceptance of the *Book of Mormon* cultures was obviously not a consideration of the Prophet.

METAL PLATES

In the nineteenth century discoveries of past cultures, most of which were being made in the Old World, were invariably being found recorded on wood, leather, or papyrus. Civil, penal, and religious laws were occasionally inscribed on metal plaques, but the ancient Greeks and Romans who did that used the more common parchment or papyrus when compiling their books. As late as the mid-twentieth century, experts continued to accept the thesis that metal was never used in book production. David Diringer, an expert in the field of ancient writings, states in *The Hand-Produced Book*, published in 1953, that "as far as we know, metal was never used for book production in the ordinary sense of the term" (Diringer, p.50).

The only known "books" found in the New World before 1830 were the Mayan codices made from bark paper and skins, and most of them had been destroyed by the Spaniards. A couple of surviving examples were sent to Europe by Cortez in 1519.

Only common sense would suggest that anyone intent on revealing to the world a "book" compiled centuries in the past would make use of the most recent knowledge and report this book as being made of either wood, paper (bark, etc.) or animal skins. Why select a material that to an expert like Mr. Diringer, writing over a century later, could still declare was never used for book production?

Now ancient writings on metal are being discovered every few years. When, in 1887, Martin T. Lamb published an anti-Mormon book attacking the possible existence of metal plates such as those Joseph recovered from Hill Cumorah, he was merely reflecting the knowledge available to common people such as Joseph Smith in 1830. In his book *The Golden Bible; Or, The Book of Mormon. Is It From God?*, Lamb made a charge characteristic of most critics of the *Book of Mormon* in the nineteenth century, when he flatly stated "no such records were ever engraved upon golden plates, or any other plates, in the early ages" (Lamb, p. 11).

Since Joseph Smith's unique report of the plates in a stone box, more than fifty stone boxes have been found in the Americas alone, containing valuable articles, including written records. More than sixty sets of metal plates containing writings have been found worldwide. These finds constitute one of the most dramatic examples of one of Joseph Smith's claims sustained by later scientific evidence (Cheesman, pp. 77-82).

BOUNTIFUL

The end of Lehi's trek in Saudi Arabia before embarking for America more than 2500 years ago was a lush coastal area that provided trees large enough for shipbuilding. Incredibly, the southern coast of the Arabian peninsula, 1400 miles long, contains only one place that perfectly fits the description provided in the Book of Nephi - and this is Salalah, a fertile oasis-like bay only twenty-eight-miles long and seven-miles wide. Westerners did not rediscover this area until the 1920s, almost eighty years after the Prophet Joseph's death. Everything at this jumping off place for Lehi and his family perfectly dovetails – from large trees and wild honey to iron ore and high cliffs. There was no way a nineteenth-century American could have known that such a place existed along the 1400-mile-long desert coastline of Saudi Arabia, except by information gathered from a manuscript written by ancient travelers who had been there (Hilton, pp. 24-40).

CHIASMI

This is a common literary form used by ancient Hebrews in which a verse or elements of several verses, once stated, are repeated in reverse order. It was done by ancient writers to enhance memorization. Knowledge of this often complex literary form had been almost totally lost to modern scholars by the nineteenth century. It was again discovered and studied in the mid-nineteenth century in Great Britain, but it was scholarly knowledge – strictly unavailable to Joseph Smith in Palmyra in 1829.

In fact, it was not discovered in the *Book of Mormon* until the 1960s when it was found by a graduate student at Brigham Young University. It was discovered that the entire Book of Mosiah, the thirty-sixth chapter of Alma, and the entire Book of First Nephi are in chiasmic form. In addition, there are numerous shorter chiasmi throughout the *Book of Mormon*. Such a discovery amounts to striking evidence of the *Book of Mormon* being a genuine ancient document with a Hebrew background. This one discovery alone reduces the possibility of this 500-page epic being a nineteenth-century fraud to almost zero (Wallace, pp. 105-12).

EARTH DIVIDED

The Bible makes a brief reference to a division of the earth in Genesis 10:25 concerning Peleg, in whose days "was the earth divided." Little was made of this rather ambiguous verse, however, until Joseph Smith received a clarifying revelation in 1831. In the D&C 133:20-24, the Lord reveals some of the events that will occur at His second coming when "He shall command the great deep, and it shall be driven back into the north countries, and the islands shall become one land.... and the earth shall be like it was in the days before it was divided."

Previously, Bible scholars believed the "division" referred to a division of the family of Eber, father of Peleg. The Doctrine and Covenants makes it quite evident, however, that the "division" was of what was once one single land mass.

It was not until sixty-eight years after the death of the Prophet that a scientist by the name of Alfred Wegener first set forth this same concept, naming the undivided land mass Pangaea. Then, in the 1960s, evidence of this theory was confirmed with the discovery of the Continental Drift, in which it was established that the Eastern and Western hemispheres are slowly drifting away from each other. Their division "in the days of Peleg" is also evidenced by the geographic "fit" of their coastlines (Brough & Griffin, pp. 64-65).

CREATION EX NIHILO

Almost without exception fundamentalist Christians believe in ex nihilo (from nothing) creation. More liberal Christian bodies are still ignoring or only timidly taking a second look at this traditional belief that can be traced to St. Augustine: "Because therefore God made all things which he did not beget of himself, not of those things that did not exist at all, that is, of nothing . . . for there was not anything of which he could make them" (Augustine, chap. 26). This doctrine was and still is quite universally accepted among most faiths today because it serves to dramatically demonstrate the power of the Christian God. Refuting such a well-established doctrine was not only irrational in the 1830s, but bordered on blasphemy since it implied a limitation of God's omnipotence.

However, on Sunday, April 7, 1844, during a Nauvoo sermon honoring his friend King Follett who had been accidentally killed the previous month, Joseph Smith astonished his followers with the following observation concerning the traditional belief in creation ex nihilo: "The 'word' create ....does not mean to create out of nothing; it means to organize .... the pure principles of element are

92

principles which can never be destroyed; they may be organized and re-organized, but not destroyed. They had no beginning and can have no End" (Burton, pp. 344-45).

This necessity of pre-existent materials in the creation of anything and the eternal permanence of the elements has been universally accepted in all scientific circles today. And even in a few theological circles, it has gained acceptance by those who claim God only works within established scientific laws.

SPACE DISCOVERIES

On March 20, 1839, while a prisoner in Liberty jail in Missouri, Joseph pronounced an amazing prophesy of what would be revealed by scientists in our times: "And also, if there be bounds set to the heavens or to the seas, or to the dry land, or to the sun, moon, or stars - All the times of their revolutions, all the appointed days, months, and years, and all the days of their days, months, and years, and all their glories, laws, and set times, shall be revealed in the days of the dispensation of the fullness of times" (DC, 121:30-31).

The "days of the dispensation of the fullness of time" began with the establishment of the Church in 1830 and is the period of time in which we now live. Consider all that has been recently discovered in oceanography, geology, and space exploration. And then compare this wealth of findings with the knowledge of these things in 1839 or even the likelihood of the fulfillment of such a prophesy when interest, effort, and resources were directed toward westward settlement and building homes and communities and certainly not toward such "unrevealable" and non – important realms as space and undersea exploration. It is only when put into the context of existing knowledge and interest in 1839 that such an astounding prophesy, uttered in a darkened dungeon in a remote frontier village in Missouri, takes on such remarkable significance.

SPECIFIC PROPHECIES

Many of Joseph's prophecies were of an even more specific nature. One of the first of such prophecies revealed occurred when he noted what the angel Moroni told him on the night of September 21, 1823. Although initially stated by Moroni, Joseph became the mouthpiece of that heavenly being and thus the prophet who informed his fellow beings "that my name would be had for good and evil spoken of among all people" (*Joseph Smith -- History*, 2:33). For an obscure farm boy in an upstate New York frontier community to suggest such a future for himself would have been an incredibly presumptuous and nonsensical risk, unless the prophesy actually was from the Lord.

From that date until his death in 1844, Joseph pronounced numerous prophecies. Duane S. Crowther compiled a list of 141 such prophecies in his book, *The Prophecies of Joseph Smith*, published in 1963. Most of these prophecies have already been fulfilled or are in the process of fulfillment and range from foretelling the growth of the Lord's Church in these latter days to the coming of the Civil War twenty-eight years before it began, even prophesying where its outbreak would occur. He even foretold the calling of the Confederate States upon Great Britain for help during this conflict.

One of the most interesting prophecies was voiced during Joseph's incarceration in the Liberty jail after the Saints were ordered expelled from Missouri. Upon hearing that his attorney, Alexander Doniphan, considered accepting some Jackson County land in payment for a debt from a client, Joseph advised him against it. Because the Saints had been so ruthlessly expelled from Jackson County, Joseph prophesied to Doniphan that God's wrath hung over that land and the attorney would "live to see the day when it will be visited by fire and sword." During the Civil War a quarter of a century later, because of the depredations of Missouri Confederate partisans, the Union Army issued the infamous General Order #11, which forcibly expelled 20,000 citizens from four Missouri counties, including Jackson, and destroyed their crops and burned their homes. This was the most drastic measure taken against civilians in a compact area during the Civil War and was implemented in a Union state.

Joseph also foresaw the driving of the Saints to the Rocky Mountains but prophesied he would not be in their number. He accurately predicted the political future of such leaders as Martin Van Buren and Stephen A. Douglas. He accurately prophesied the future of such associates as Dan Jones, Willard Richards, Orson Hyde, Brigham Young, and Porter Rockwell, not living to see all of those prophecies literally fulfilled. And finally, though he had been in numerous situations where his life was in jeopardy, it was not until the final days before the Carthage assassinations that he stated that if he and Hyrum were ever taken again they would be murdered. On his way to Carthage, he again prophesied his murder and that it would be said of him, "He was murdered in cold blood."

The foretelling of future events must eventually be proven true or false and is not a safe course for any false prophet, but to foretell one's own demise in an impending event is a guaranteed way of demonstrating a prophetic calling. Joseph had nothing to prove however – he was merely preparing his people for a reality for which the Lord was preparing him.

95

ABANDONING FAMILIAR GROUND

In his book *A Storyteller in Zion: Essays and Speeches,* Orson Scott Card makes some interesting observations on the Book of Mormon. Joseph Smith was not a military strategist and although he dressed in a Nauvoo Legion uniform and attended parades and displays, he showed no inclination or flair in planning military campaigns or talking about military matters. He had followers such as John Bennett and Sampson Avard who were far more involved and to whom Joseph was far more inclined to leave such matters. And yet one of the first things investigators note when reading the *Book of Mormon* is the heavy emphasis on wars and battles, especially by writers such as Mormon and Moroni. It is illogical that the author of such descriptive military literature would have shown so little interest in the same subject in his daily communications and writings. For Joseph to dwell at such length on an unfamiliar and apparently unappealing subject would have certainly increased the likelihood of revealable flaws by those far more knowledgeable in that area.

On the other hand, why not dwell more on a subject that any young man in the early nineteenth century was interested in, and according to the Prophet's critics, which he himself was more familiar with – women? It is difficult to read any literature – books, newspapers, or periodicals of the early 1800s – that do not dwell at some length on the role of women and romantic love. Perhaps their roles would not be politically correct by modern standards, but women were certainly not ignored in that romantic era. Where, however, are the women in the *Book of Mormon*? Where are the love stories that were a part of everyday life in Joseph's America or even in the Bible? On only three occasions are *Book of Mormon* women given names – Sariah, Isabel and Abish – whereas the Bible has several stories of love such as David and Bathsheba, Samson and Delilah, and Jacob and Leah.

Ignoring the familiar and dwelling on the unfamiliar is a perilous route to devising hard-to-refute historical fabrications. It was obviously not Joseph's choice; he was merely the translator of historical records. One cannot help imagining what went through the Prophet's mind as the details of such unfamiliar history and culture unfolded before his eyes. One of the things that probably did not occur to him was the prospect of so many future critics believing that he, a young unlettered farmer's son in a remote frontier community, could conceivably have devised such a detailed and complex epic himself. They might for awhile question its origin, but to credit him with fraudulently spawning such a Homeric narrative would become a major frustration, tempered perhaps by the thought that his critics really believed him capable of such an irrefutable masterpiece of ancient literature.

CHAPTER X

WOULD HAVE RECEIVED REVELATIONS IN SECRET

I waive the quantum o'the sin,
The hazard of concealing;
- Robert Burns

Throughout history, devotees of various religious leaders have accepted the spiritual manifestations claimed by the elect, even in the absence of witnesses. Buddha became the "enlightened" founder of a major world faith through solitary meditation, acceptable to millions who considered him a wise leader. Mohammed received his "commission" from an angel in a desert cave around A.D. 610 just as he received many of the teachings of Allah – alone and during the night. Even many of the revelations and manifestations found in the Bible and believed by millions were never witnessed by anyone other than the claimant. Examples are Jacob's vision of the ladder to heaven; Moses and the burning bush; Daniel, alone, seeing and talking with the Lord; and Jacob being visited by the Lord who sends him into Egypt with is family. The entire Book of Revelation received by John was witnessed only by him. Bible believers even accept revelations and visions by non-prophets such a Cornelius who saw and talked with an angel, and Balaam who met with God and received instruction.

Well aware of such precedents as these, Joseph Smith would have stood on far firmer ground to have received his revelations in solitary. Why, when such solitary visions and revelations were so universally believed by millions, would he have risked exposure by going "public" with his communications with God or his heavenly agents? Why – unless Joseph was so confident in the authenticity of those revelations that "exposure" never entered his mind?

If such a sharing of these spiritual manifestations had been limited to one or two instances, critics might be justified in chalking them up to hallucinations or delusions, but they occurred repeatedly and with a variety of individuals, especially during the formative years of the Restoration.

It is especially revealing to note the manner in which Joseph received revelations as observed by these persons. Parley P. Pratt, present on several such occasions, leaves us a description of one particular revelation that became Section 50 of the Doctrine and Covenants, received in May of 1831 at Kirtland, Ohio:

> After we had joined in prayer in his translating room, he
> dictated in our presence the following revelation: -- (Each
> sentence was uttered slowly and very distinctly, and with
> a pause between each, sufficiently long for it to be recorded,
> by an ordinary writer, in long hand.
>
> This was the manner in which all his written revelations
> were dictated and written. There was never any hesitation
> reviewing, or reading back. (Pratt, P. P., p.62).

William E. McLellin, another close associate, likewise recalled:

> I as scribe, have written revelations from the mouth of
> (the Prophet). And I have been present many times
> when others wrote for Joseph; therefore I speak as
> one having experience. The scribe seats himself at a
> desk or table, with pen, ink, and paper. The subject
> of inquiry being understood, the Prophet and Revelator
> inquires of God. He spiritually sees, hears, and feels,
> and then speaks as he is moved upon by the Holy Ghost . . .

sentence after sentence, and waits for his amanuenses to write. (Backman & Cowan, p.2).

It is of interest to note that McLellin, who later apostatized from the Church, revealed to Orson Pratt in a letter twenty-two years later the full significance of those revelations from the Lord. He wrote, "I learned to know the voice of the Spirit of God clothed in words. And if I had heeded its voice from that day to this, I should have missed many – very many difficulties through which I have passed" (Shipps & Welch, p. 301).

During a Church Conference held in November, 1831, the Lord revealed what is now Section 1 of the D&C. Oliver Cowdery left us an account of what happened on that day: "A committee had been appointed to draft a preface... the Conference then requested Joseph to inquire of the Lord about it, and he said that he would if the people would bow in prayer with him. ... When they arose, Joseph dictated by the Spirit the preface found in the Book of Doctrine and Covenants while sitting by a window of the room ... and Sidney Rigdon wrote it down" (Backman & Cowan, p.2).

At such times as these, the only physical manifestation of the experience appeared to be a change in Joseph's countenance. Anson Call said his face became a living brilliant white. Brigham Young, one of his closest associates, recalled that Joseph's appearance, when he was under the Spirit of Revelation, was obvious to all who were in attendance; that at such times there was a peculiar clearness and transparency in his face (JD, 9:89). Such descriptions of the Prophet Joseph in such a spiritual mode is comparable to the description of Moses when he came down from Mount Sinai, as described in Exodus 34:30: "And when Aaron and all the children of Israel saw Moses, behold, the skin of his face shone;

and they were afraid to come nigh him."

It is also of interest to note here that few Christians would accuse Moses of fraud simply because Moses had no others with him to witness the writing by the Lord upon the tablets of stone. And yet on numerous occasions, Joseph had associates and at times entire assemblies to witness the writing of revelations as they came from the Lord himself through his mouthpiece. Let's examine some of those occasions by reviewing who was present at the setting for several of the revelations recorded in the Doctrine and Covenants.

Section 13 is the prayer pronounced upon the heads of Joseph Smith and Oliver Cowdery as they received the Aaronic Priesthood under the hands of the resurrected John the Baptist in May of 1829. Although Oliver later apostatized from the Church, he never denied having been a participant in this marvelous manifestation. The witnessing of and participation in such a divine experience has been granted to few individuals in the world's history and was certainly not an event that Joseph could have arranged without involvement by the Lord himself.

Eleven months later the Church was formally organized in the log house of Peter Whitmer in Fayette, New York. According to Peter's son David, approximately fifty persons were present on that April day in 1830 when Joseph received the revelation constituting section 21 of the Doctrine and Covenants.

On September 26, 1830, a general conference was called to meet again in the Whitmer home. This conference was the result of a revelation (D&C 29) received a few days previously, which Joseph considered of such importance that the full membership should learn the import of the revelation. At the time of the receipt of that revelation, just previous to the conference, Joseph was in the presence of six elders.

In January of 1831 the third general conference was held at Fayette. At this conference, Joseph received a revelation commanding the New York Saints to dispose of their homes and property and move to Ohio. The receipt of this revelation, Section 38, was described by Orson Pratt in a discourse delivered in the Salt Lake Tabernacle in 1878 in which he described the revelation as being "given before a general conference, and written by a scribe in presence of the conference " (JD 20:14).

On February 9 of that same year, the "Law of the Church" revelation recorded in Section 42, instructing members of the Church to consecrate their property for the support of the poor, was received in the presence of twelve elders. Three months later Orson Pratt was present at Thompson, Ohio, when the Prophet received the revelation that now constitutes Section 51 of the Doctrine and Covenants. This revelation which made a promise of eternal life to those Saints who obeyed the previous revelation on consecration, was described in the *Millennial Star* on August 11, 1874, as it was remembered by brother Pratt: "No great noise or physical manifestation was made; Joseph was as calm as the morning sun" (*Millennial Star*, Number 32, p.498).

It was obvious from this description that Joseph was making no attempt to give the occasion an appearance of a heavenly manifestation or anything more than what it was -- merely the Lord using him as an instrument for instruction to the Saints. Joseph himself described the undramatic receipt of that revelation at a conference of the Twelve at Commerce (later Nauvoo) in June, 1839:

> A person may profit by noticing the first intimation of
> the spirit of revelation; for instance, when you feel pure
> intelligence flowing into you, it may give you sudden

strokes of ideas, so that by noticing it, you may find
it fulfilled the same day or soon; (i.e.) those things
what were presented unto your minds by the Spirit of
God, will come to pass; and thus by learning the Spirit
of God and understanding it, you may grow into the
principle of revelation, until you become perfect in
Christ Jesus. (HC, 3:381)

This was the process of receiving most of the Lord's instructions, whether
alone or in the company of others, as was the case of Section 75, received in the
presence of an entire conference at Amherst, Ohio, on January 25, 1832. There
were times, however, when the revelation was received in a different manner, as
was the case with Section 76. But even this change in manner of receipt was still
often shared with others as Joseph did with Sidney Rigdon at Hiram, Ohio. On
that winter day at the Johnson farm home, Sidney was privileged to participate in
the vision of the degrees of glory. Although at least a dozen others were present
in the translating room and felt the power, only Sidney participated in this vision,
which Joseph described as showing every law, commandment, and promise
"touching the destiny of man" (HC 1:252-53). To those present Joseph would
describe and Elder Rigdon would verify the scenes that passed before their eyes.
Elder Rigdon stayed up the entire night writing what the two had witnessed and
what now makes up one of the most enlightening doctrines in modern scripture.

An equally glorious vision was recorded on April 3, 1836, when the
Prophet, along with Oliver Cowdery, retired behind the veil on the west side of
the Kirtland Temple. After arising from prayer, four successive visions were
opened to the pair. First Christ appeared to accept the Temple and then Moses

appeared to commit the keys of the gathering, Elias the keys of the dispensation of the Gospel of Abraham, and finally Elijah, the keys of the sealing powers (D&C 110).

It must be remembered that in the case of both of these revelations given by way of visions, Joseph's companions to the visions later apostatized but never denied that to which they had been witnesses. Why did Joseph, however, take such a chance with this risky approach to revelation if it was not entirely authentic? Not only was Joseph incapable of contriving such a vision, but the risk of later denial by a disgruntled associate was simply too significant. It is one thing to reveal you have received a vision, but it is something entirely different to share such a vision, agreeing in all details, unless it actually occurred.

Joseph's lack of hesitancy about having witnesses to his revelations, as well as sharing his revelations through visions, was certainly not characteristic of a charlatan or a glory-seeking pretender. Making use of a variety of revelatory methods, and again having witnesses to them also as in the case of the use of the Urim and Thummin (D&C 3,6, & 7), is not what one involved in fraud would have done. Not only would it have been a far less assailable route to receive revelations in solitude, but such an individual would logically have adhered to a consistent and time-proven method – the most credible and least refutable being that of inspiration by the Holy Ghost.

The crucial question therefore seems to be, "Why were so many of the Prophet's revelations witnessed by others when it was so unnecessary?" Were those early members so gullible or credulous that they were unlikely to question such revelations? If that had been their nature, most of them would not have been so distrustful or unbelieving of the religious doctrines they had grown up with.

As was pointed out in chapter 7, the early converts to the Church, especially those who gravitated to leadership positions and became the close associates of Joseph, were men of learning and intelligence, many of them from former professions that required more than average intellectual abilities and who were respected in their communities. Such individuals were not inclined to accept "supernatural" or extraordinary spiritual manifestations without reasonable evidence. In the first Quorum of the Twelve, organized in Ohio in 1835, we find four members who became state or territorial legislators, four who became teachers or noted lecturers, a lawyer, two who practiced medicine, and a successful inventor. These are not the types of professions characterized by ignorant or simple-minded individuals. And these were certainly not the type of men a pretender would attempt to deceive with imaginary revelations. What is most significant is that among these associates and of the literally hundreds who actually witnessed the receiving of revelations by the Prophet, none, including those who later apostatized and became his bitter enemies, ever disputed the heavenly manifestations they had witnessed of the Lord speaking through Joseph Smith.

And, finally, we must not overlook the divine law of witnesses: "In the mouths of two or three witnesses shall every word be established" (2 Cor.13:1). Just as the Lord provided witnesses to the Book of Mormon plates, he seemingly made arrangements for the world to be apprised of the witnesses to the revelations in the Doctrine and Covenants. At a conference held at Hiram, Ohio, on November 1, 1831, the revelations now comprising D&C 1 and known as the Preface was received. At this same conference the decision was made to publish 10,000 copies (later reduced to 3,000) of the *Book of Commandments*. Then, because of some possible questions about the wording and perhaps credibility of some of the revelations, "Joseph asked the Conference what testimony they were willing to attach to these commandments which should shortly by sent to the world" (Cannon & Cook, p.27). When several of the brethren responded that they were willing to testify that they knew they were from the Lord, Joseph received another revelation in the form of a "Testimony" by those present. This may have been signed with the intention of inclusion in the Book of Commandments, but because the mobs destroyed the printing establishment before the *Book of Commandments* was completed, we don't know for sure. Whatever the case, we do know that the elders at the Hiram Conference, according to the recorded minutes, testified that they knew the revelations were of the Lord.

That assembled witnesses were not necessarily present at every revelation does not negate the law of witnesses. Their presence on such numerous occasions and their testimonies is substantial confirmation of the Lord using Joseph as a mouthpiece for his communications. The challenge to the world by believers of this confirmation is to find in the annals of history any claim comparable to Joseph Smith's calling as a prophet, that had so many contemporary witnesses (and with no retractions), but that is still challenged by so many. Tradition truly can be the greatest hindrance to reason.

CHAPTER XI

WOULD HAVE ACTED AS A PROPHET

He seems to employ no studied effort to guard
himself against misrepresentations, but often leaves
himself exposed to misconstruction by those who
watch for his faults.
- (Letter written by Orson Spencer in 1842)

Perhaps the reason so many Christians believe the heavens are closed and

God no longer communicates to us today through such men as Moses and

Abraham is because there is no one who fits the proper mold to receive his

communications. Does God require someone with the proper appearance and

demeanor to be his spokesman to mankind? Is that the reason Joseph Smith, who

spurned attempts to cast himself in such a role, is rejected as a Prophet by so

many? Some of his devotees have tried to characterize him as a traditional Old

Testament Prophet in spite of the more obvious dissimilarities.

Truman Madsen, in his 1965 book, *Joseph Smith Among the Prophets*,

compared Joseph to what he referred to as "widely accepted descriptions of the

great prophets of the Hebrew-Christian tradition" (Madsen, p.47) and noted that in

these comparisons Joseph qualified as a true Prophet. Madsen's arguments are

persuasive, but that doesn't mean Joseph qualified to fit the stereotype in the

minds of the average early nineteenth-century American. In discussing how a

nineteenth-century religious fraud would have been inclined to present himself in

the most plausible manner to an American audience, this becomes a significant

and telling point.

With his education and knowledge of the characteristics of ancient

prophets being far more limited than that of Brother Madsen, Joseph was far more aware of the conventional image in the minds of his family, friends, and neighbors when the word "prophet" was mentioned, and that stereotype was not much different than it would be to the average person today. J. B. Newhall gave a lecture in Salem, Massachusetts, from which a quote was reproduced in the *Nauvoo Neighbor* on June 21, 1843. In a conversation he claimed to have had with the Prophet Joseph Smith, he remarked, "He is a jolly fellow; and according to his view is one of the last persons on earth whom God would have raised up a prophet or priest, he is so diametrically opposite to that which he ought to be, in order to merit the titles or to act in said offices" (Hill, p. 10).

A real prophet, most people believe, must first of all look like a prophet – older, solemn, and, of course, with a beard. He must talk like a prophet, using Biblical language in a reserved, articulate manner filled with allegories and symbolism. He must also have the serious, ascetic, and joyless demeanor of an Old Testament prophet. Finally, he must do something about that name Smith. He couldn't help being born with that name, but he certainly was aware it might be held against him as an insult to religious sensibility.

It would therefore be only logical that a young pretender to the title of Prophet in nineteenth-century America, with even a superficial knowledge of the Bible, would be aware of the custom of name changing found in those scriptures. In the New Testament Saul become Paul, and in the Old Testament we find the Lord renaming Abram as Abraham and Jacob as Israel.

There appears to be no evidence that either the Lord or Joseph considered a name change for this American prophet with such a common American name. As a result, the unimpressive name of Smith did become justification for attacking his credibility. In the anti-Mormon novel, *House of Shame*, we find a character making reference to Joseph's humble family name: "'Smith!' said Miss Priscilla, with a snort' That's a fine name for a prophet, isn't it?'" (Pidgin, p.90).

Contemporaries of Joseph, with pretensions of religious greatness and aware of how powerful a thing a name can be, did change their names. In November of 1835, the Prophet Joseph was visited in Kirtland by a bearded and long-haired man who introduced himself by the name of Joshua, who conversed with Joseph on religious doctrine. Brother Smith finally ascertained that "Joshua" was in reality Robert Matthias, another name for Robert Mathews, who was recently released from prison back in New York. Mathews had served time there on a variety of charges, including suspicion of poisoning some of his disciples with arsenic-laced blackberries. Two days after his arrival in Kirtland, Joseph ordered him to leave, saying in his journal that he had "for once, cast out the devil in bodily shape" (HC, 2:304-7).

Even the name Joseph, as Biblical as it was, was used to mock what the critics believed were his prophetic pretensions. His enemies seemed to delight in referring to him as "Joe," occasionally in his presence. When Josiah Quincy, the mayor of Boston, visited Nauvoo shortly before the Prophet's death, a Methodist minister, whose name Quincy could not later recall, was in his party. During discussions on theology, Joseph had apparently bested the clergyman all day long. Finally, the preacher resorted to insult, telling Joseph that in a discussion on some false doctrine, he had told his congregation that they might as well believe Joe Smith as that!

Joseph's response demonstrated unruffled superiority as he asked the minister if he had really used the name "Joe Smith" in a Sunday sermon. When the divine said he had and why not, Joseph replied, "Well, considering only the day and place, it would have been more respectful to have said Lieutenant General Joseph Smith" (Cannon, George Q., p. 349). The Prophet well understood the value of humor as a defensive weapon.

Just as Joseph appeared disinterested in improving his image as a prophet by changing his name, he was equally disinclined to change his looks, in spite of any advantage it might have brought him in being accepted as a real prophet.

Henry Brown, author of an Illinois history that was published the year of Joseph and Hyrum's martyrdoms, met the Prophet, and in his history seemed to bristle with disillusionment: "He is, upon the whole, an ordinary man; and considering his pretensions, a very ordinary man" (Brown, p. 120). Joseph had seemed somewhat amused back in Kirtland in 1835 when he was introduced to a man from the East. The Prophet recalled that "After hearing my name, he remarked that I was nothing but a man, indicating by this expression, that he supposed that a person to whom the Lord should see fit to reveal His will, must be something more than a man" (HC, 2:302).

A few years later, a reporter from the *Boston Bee* newspaper described his impressions upon meeting Joseph Smith in Nauvoo. In an article in 1843 he wrote: " . . . long before I heard of the Prophet Joseph Smith, and indeed before he had existence, I had formed some very curious ideas about ancient prophets.". He went on to describe the stereotype of an Old Testament prophet with long gray beard, dressed in animal skins, and living in caves and dens of the earth. The reporter, who classified himself as an infidel, wrote that when he met Joseph Smith however, he "could not help noticing that he dressed, talked and acted like other men, and in every respect exactly the opposite of what I had conjured up in my imagination a prophet" (HC, 5:407-8).

Robert Richards, author of an anti-Mormon book in 1854, noted that a man of Smith's pretensions should at least look like Isaiah (Richards, p. 60).

Even Thomas Ford, governor of Illinois, whom many consider responsible for Joseph's death through his negligence in taking the proper precautions in seeing to the safety of the prisoners incarcerated in the Carthage jail, recognized how different Joseph was from the traditional stereotype of a prophet: "It must not be supposed that the pretended Prophet practiced the tricks of a common impostor; that he was a dark and gloomy person, with a long beard, a grave and severe aspect, and a reserved and saintly carriage of his person; on the contrary he was full of levity, even to boyish rompings" (Ford, 2:213-14).

Joseph's writings and language also reveal a disinclination to conform to the pattern expected of prophets or visionary divines. William Blake, the well-known English poet and a contemporary of Joseph Smith, combined the role of prophet and poet. His prophetic visionary experiences were filled with symbolism and allegories like other visionary religious leaders of the time, as was expected of anyone speaking as a prophet. Emanuel Swedenborg, another eminent divine in the century preceding Joseph, also wrote and preached in the manner expected of such visionaries. In describing Christ Swedenborg saw him at a distance "either before the right eye or before the left eye. Before the right eye He appeared exactly like the Sun, in splendor and magnitude like the sun of this world; but before the left eye He does not appear as a sun but as the moon" (Swedenborg, p. 51). Joseph on the other hand, saw him like us – a man!

Brigham Young, who often observed Joseph's receipt of revelations, made the following observation on language and revelation: "When God speaks to the people, he does it in a manner to suit their circumstance and capacities. . . Should the Lord Almighty send an angel to re-write the Bible, it would in many places be very different from what it is now" (JD 9:311).

Although Joseph, so familiar with Biblical style, often phrased his revelations in a similar manner, it was never to the extent, that critics then and even now believe is sufficient to be evidence of the Lord speaking. His revelations are couched, in spite of some King James phraseology, in only the simple and unadorned prose considered essential for imparting the necessary information. An example of this is the Pearl of Great Price in which Joseph describes the visit of John the Baptist in only one verse saying "While we were thus employed, praying and calling upon the Lord, a messenger from heaven descended in a cloud of light, and having laid his hands upon us, he ordained us" (JS History, 1:68). Oliver Cowdery, a participant on that occasion, later described the same event in the *Messenger and Advocate* in a much lengthier version using such phrases as "from the midst of eternity, the voice of the Redeemer spake peace to us . . . from the glitter of the May Sun beam, which then shed its brilliancy over the face of nature! . . . while His love enkindled upon our souls, and we were rapt in the vision of the Almighty!" (*Messenger & Advocate*, V.1, Oct., 1934, p.16)

Joseph was himself aware of what some might consider language deficiencies in the wording of his revelations. This is evidenced in the revelations recorded at a Hiram, Ohio, conference in November 1831: "Your eyes have been upon my servant Joseph Smith, Jun., and his language you have known, and his imperfections you have known; and you have sought in your heart knowledge that you might express beyond his language; this you also know" (D&C 67:5). The revelation then challenged Joseph's followers to choose the wisest among them to attempt to write something comparable to the revelations received by Joseph. William McLellin, it was recorded, tried and failed. It was not because he could not write as well as Joseph, but it was obvious to all assembled that the Spirit of the Lord itself was manifested only in what Joseph dictated and was noticeably lacking in the words of McLellin.

There was nothing pretentious, as would be characteristic of a pretender, in either his writings or his public speaking. Just as the reporter from the *Boston Bee* was amazed by Joseph's attire and looking like other men, he was also apparently astonished by his speaking. He had expected to see a prophet living in the wilderness as John the Baptist, venturing forth only when he had a message from heaven and then he would cry out "with so much sanctity, that everybody would know he was a prophet" (HC, 5:407). If the Lord's ways are not our ways, however, neither are a prophet's ways what we think they should be.

At one of the Nauvoo lyceums, Mercy Thompson heard Joseph speak: "I have listened to his clear and masterly explanations of deep and difficult questions. To him all things seemed simple and easy to be understood, and thus he could make them plain to others as no other man could" (Ehat,xx).

Just as the teachings of Christ were made plain only to those who were spiritually prepared to receive them, so must the words of a prophet be found acceptable only to those spiritually receptive, as were such individuals as Parley Pratt. He described the Prophet's language as "abounding in original eloquence peculiar to himself – not polished – not studied – not smoothed and softened by education and refined by art; but flowing forth in its own native simplicity . . . none listened to him that were ever weary with his discourse"(Andrus, p.13). And, just as was the case with his name, appearance,and language not being in accord with the traditional image of a prophet, his demeanor was even less so. His refusal to play the part of an Old Testament prophet in his deportment was unsettling, if not to say disappointing, to critics or even to members; it occasionally being a factor in their apostasy from the Church. One of the very first apostates was a former Methodist preacher, Ezra Booth, who left the Church not long after his conversion in 1831 in Kirtland. In a letter to Edward Partridge, a faithful member, Booth wrote at the time of his apostasy: "Have you not frequently observed in Joseph, a want of that sobriety, prudence, and stability which are some of the prominent traits of the Christian character? Have you not discovered in him, a spirit of lightness and levity, a temper of mind easily irritated, and an habitual proneness to Jesting and joking?" (Hill, p.8).

George A. Smith recalled a family in Kirtland that apostatized because while on a visit to his home, they observed Joseph "came down out of the translating room, where he had been translating by the gift and power of God, and commenced playing with his little children" (JD, 2:214). Apparently such a couple could not picture Abraham or Moses or any Biblical personage playing with their children, just as there are critics today who fault Joseph for being too "common."

If the church that Joseph was an instrument in restoring to the earth teaches as the ultimate purpose of mankind's existence, the fullness of joy, certainly the Prophet's delight in playing with his children should be evidence of his prophetic calling, not a judgment against it. His love of all children was one of his most often reported characteristics and not something he could disguise for the purpose of appearing more grave or serious in keeping with the Biblical stereotypes.

In both Kirtland and Nauvoo, when members from the countryside arrived for meetings, Joseph was often seen moving from wagon to wagon, greeting his brothers and sisters, especially noticing the children and taking them by the hand. Once when Emma lost a baby, a neighbor "loaned" Joseph a twin baby girl to help Emma through her initial grief. Joseph would pick up the baby each morning and return it each night. Later, when that baby died, Joseph grieved like it had been one of his own. For those who thought Joseph's love for children was excessive, the response by his followers was an emphatic NO! It was evidence of the nobility of his soul and a manifestation of his special calling as the Lord's representative.

The Prophet's "unprophet-like" demeanor was not limited to just his relationship to children. He enjoyed and excelled at such common sports of the frontier as "catch-as-catch-can" wrestling (free style), pulling sticks, jumping at a mark, or target shooting. The Prophet's oldest son remembered visiting the Red Brick Store as a boy to find that his father "had spent most of the afternoon wrestling with customers. The grassy turf outside the store had been dug up and stomped down by the wrestlers and excited spectators" (Givens, p.156).

A more reserved and prophet-like demeanor, logic would suggest, would have impressed visitors and investigators alike, but it was not Joseph's way, especially with the insincere or pompous. Wilford Woodruff recalled a visit two ministers made to the Prophet's home in Nauvoo, obviously with the intention of satisfying their preconceived notions of him as a fraud. At the end of the visit, as they walked outside with Joseph, he made a mark on the ground with his boot and then jumped to it. Turning to his startled but pretentious guests, he asked, "Which one of you can beat that?" He well knew that such unprophet-like behavior could

115

be used against him, but he was too confident in his calling to resist the discomfiture of his pious visitors" (Andrus, p.47).

Wilford himself recalled his first meeting with Joseph and, quite unlike the two ministers, was not the least put off by the common-place activity in which found the Prophet engaged. "It might have shocked the faith of some men. I found him and his brother Hyrum out shooting at a mark with a brace of pistols" (Givens, pp.155-56).

Understanding the dilemma faced by the sincere seekers of religious truths who were confused by Joseph's deviation from the orthodox Biblical prophets, Joseph took time to patiently enlighten. In his journal for February 8, 1843, he recorded: "This morning I read German, and visited with a brother and sister from Michigan, who thought that 'a prophet is always a prophet'; but I told them that a prophet was a prophet only when he was acting as such." At the end of the same paragraph, Joseph notes, "At four in the afternoon, I went out with my little Frederick, to exercise myself by sliding on the ice" (HC, 5:265).

An analysis of Joseph's unwillingness to put on the trappings of a popularly perceived prophet of the Lord actually adds to his credibility. If a true prophet is God's representative and spokesman on earth, he is obligated to be himself as God must be. If, as the scriptures tell us, to achieve life eternal "is to know Him, the only true God," it would seem a contradiction to have His spokesman be something he is not. The Lord recognized that nineteenth-century America was not the days of Abraham or Moses or David, and just as He would not have required those prophets to change their names or looks or demeanors to fit a stereotype of an earlier Adam or Enoch, he certainly would not have forced Joseph Smith into an artificial mold. If Joseph had attempted to initiate the traditionally believed role of an ancient prophet, he might have had more success with the masses of the nineteenth-century world. Certainly the temptation to appear to potential converts in the guise of what they expected and wanted to see, would have been irresistible to men of lesser spiritual understanding. If the masses do not accept Joseph as a prophet because he doesn't quite fit a superficial stereotype, however, that is their problem and not the Lord's. Joseph, understanding the mind of the Lord more than anyone else of his or our generations, was firm in his resolve to be accepted for what he truly was and not what mortal minds think he should have been.

CHAPTER XII

WOULD HAVE SHOWED GREATER
CONCERN FOR SELF-PRESERVATION

Many men are willing to give their
lives for what they believe, but what
man is willing to give his life for
something he knows is a fraud?
-Elder Artel Ricks

Self-preservation is one of the strongest impulses in human beings and becomes of lesser importance only when a more noble cause takes precedence, such as to save the lives of others, love of one's country, or for one's religious convictions. To determine whether the loss of one's life, as was the case with Joseph Smith, was truly a sacrifice for such a noble cause as a sincere faith in his religious convictions and not merely a blunder in his self-preservation efforts, we must review his entire pattern of self-preservation efforts. During his fourteen year career as Prophet and President of the Restored Church, what steps did he take to guard himself from the constant threats and actual attempts on his life from his numerous enemies? Joseph loved life and his family and had thousands who loved him. He certainly would not have risked losing his life and all its pleasures for anything less than a cause that exceeded all of that – and certainly not to give greater credence to a hoax.

In reviewing Joseph's casual approach to self-preservation, we must first deal with any efforts he made to protect himself from his enemies. Critics have pointed to his "lifeguards" as evidence that he was paranoid and took every precaution to preserve his life. Who were these "lifeguards"?

Joseph did, in fact, appoint twenty men as his "lifeguards" during the march of Zion's Camp in 1834 and another group again in the Nauvoo Legion. It is important to note, however, that this term is military terminology for escorts for high-ranking officers, such as Joseph was in both Zion's Camp and the Nauvoo Legion. At the time of his death in 1844, there were thirteen men as his bodyguard, at least nine of whom were those originally selected in 1841 when the Nauvoo Legion was organized. It appears that as more men became available in the rapidly expanding church, Joseph, rather than detailing more "guards" as a fearful "pretender" would do in a time of increasing danger, actually allowed his guard detail to diminish – allowing most of them to remain in the detail because they were part of the original Legion organization. They were therefore not men selected specifically to keep Joseph from harm but to fulfill military functions as honor guards do today. As evidence of Joseph's unwillingness to make greater use of guards, as threats against his life from enemies and apostates increased, especially during the last three years of his life, we must look at the activities of some of those nine "guards" who served him during those final three years. Were they actually guarding the Prophet as their titles might imply?

Thomas Groves served three missions during his time as bodyguard and at the time of Joseph's martyrdom was in Michigan. A. Cutler went to the Pineries in September 1841 for a year and on the day of the Martyrdom in Carthage was in Nauvoo. Reynolds Cahoon was one of the three men responsible for urging Joseph to recross the River and give himself up to the authorities. John Snyder was on a mission; he had left for England the day after Christmas in 1843. John S. Butler spent two missions to the Sioux Indians starting in 1842, after which he returned and then went to visit relatives in Kentucky. In July 1843 he was called on another mission and didn't return until the spring of 1844. It's obvious such men were guards in name only and spent little time actually protecting the life of the Prophet.

Strangely enough, incidentally, it was that same John Butler who in his autobiography mentions the fact that "Joseph's life was not safe at all. He had several lifeguards to go with him when he went anywhere" (*John Butler Autobiography*, p.27).

Although Butler was apparently not around enough to observe such precautions, it's true that the Prophet did on occasions, when danger was most imminent, use guards. He apparently knew at those times his work was not finished and it was important to live until it was. When he felt his work was completed and his life was in the gravest danger, he literally dismissed those guards. Brother Butler, who had just returned from his most recent mission, was one of those who accompanied Joseph on his final trip to Carthage. There, Joseph, aware of the danger to not only himself but his friends also, told them to return home:

> We begged him to let us stay with him and die with him, if necessary, but he said, no, we were to return to our homes. . . He blessed us and told us to go. We bade them (Joseph and Hyrum) farewell and started. We had twenty miles to ride, and we went the whole distance without uttering one word. All were dumb and still and felt the spirit as I did myself. . . I felt like the prophets of the Lord were about to be taken from us and that they were going to await their doom. (*John Butler Autobiography*, p.26)

And there were no guards to protect the Prophet on the night of March 24, 1832, at the Johnson farm at Hiram, Ohio, when a mob broke into the home where the Smiths were staying and dragged Joseph outside where they beat him, tried to poison him with a vial of nitric acid, and covered him with tar. If self-preservation had been one of his primary concerns, he would certainly have stayed secluded after that attack. The very next day, however, he publicly appeared at a previously announced baptism and proceeded to talk and baptize in the presence of several of the mobbers.

Two years later, on the Zion's' Camp march in the Spring of 1834 from Kirtland to Missouri, Joseph had selected a detachment of lifeguards. That they were primarily a military escort, however, is apparent from his making George A. Smith the "armorbearer," that being an ancient title from the days of armor wearing warriors. On that march Joseph, unlike a typical charlatan or pretender, shared all the discomforts and dangers inherent in a 900-mile march through and into hostile and unfamiliar territory. Joseph willingly shared bad food, at one time chastising Zebedee Coltrin for giving him (Joseph) good bread while some of the others were eating sour bread.

When cholera broke out in camp, Joseph, ignoring its contagious nature, tried to administer to heal the stricken, finally being hit with the disease himself.

Four years later, at Far West, Joseph was again in mortal jeopardy evidenced by the violence already done the Saints at places like Crooked River and Haun's Mill, where eighteen men and boys, ranging in age from ten to seventy-five were massacred by a militia-mob of 240.

When opportunities to escape such life-threatening situations as these occurred, Joseph often ignored them. At the time of the surrender of the Saints at Far West, immediately after the massacre at Haun's Mill, there were among the defenders a number of men who had been in the battle Crooked River. That battle, in which the Saints had driven off a mob army advancing on Far West, occurred only a week before the surrender of the Mormons at Far West. So now the mob was thirsting for the blood of those who had been at Crooked River as well as the blood of Joseph. In the night before the surrender, before the mobocrats could lay hands on them, about twenty of those battle veterans, including Joseph's brother Samuel, escaped and eventually made their way to safety in Illinois. No stigma was ever attached to these men for escaping the risk of possible death at the hands of the vengeance-seeking mob. Joseph and his close associates, who were actually sentenced to death by a court martial after the surrender, would have been totally justified in escaping with the Crooked River veterans (Bio. Ency. 1:280). Instead, Joseph remained with his people to surrender the following day and to be sentenced to death by an illegal court-martial. He and his close associates were saved only because of the dissenting actions of a Missouri militia officer, General Alexander Doniphan.

It is of interest to note that while yet in the hands of the merciless mob and three days before General Clark promised the Far West Saints in a public address that they would never see their leaders again for "their fate is fixed – their die is cast – their doom is sealed" (HC 3:202-4), Joseph prophesied to his fellow prisoner, Parley P. Pratt. Unlike his refusal to prophesy safety for himself as was the case at Carthage six years later – on November 3, 1838, he told Brother Pratt and his fellow prisoners: "Be of good cheer, Brethren; the word of the Lord came to me last night that our lives should be given us, and that whatever we may suffer during this captivity, not one of our lives should be taken" (Pratt, p.192).

Not only would a charlatan have been disinclined to promise sanctuary in such a life-threatening situation, his major concern would have been the seeking of self-preservation. Life, to any rational person, is far more important than the maintenance of a ruse.

Let us move on, however, to the most convincing segment of his life in regard to his readiness to forfeit it. There is only one impulse in life that is stronger than the self-profit motive and that is the preservation of life. The maintenance of a hoax is not even close in preeminence. The crucial question appears to therefore be – did Joseph Smith really believe his death in Carthage was imminent? If not, then his detractors can legitimately cast him, in this respect, in the category of an ordinary pretender who analyzed the danger he was in and felt it insignificant compared to the advantage of continuing the fraud. On the other hand, if he was totally convinced of his impending death and yet did not take the available steps to avoid it, then his critics should re-evaluate their judgments of the genuineness of the prophetic calling that led Joseph to an avoidable martyrdom. We can certainly dismiss any suggestions that he had a death wish or was suicidal. He loved life and the joys it brought him in spite of his persecutions, and he loved his family. His sorrow and tears in parting from them for the last time were sincere and his assertions of wishing to see them again and preach to his people again were genuine. He went to his death reluctantly but knowingly.

Joseph was martyred at the age of thirty-eight and a half. While in the Liberty jail in Missouri, five years before his death, Lyman Wight "said that Joseph told him he would not live to see forty years" (HC 7:212).

Three years and nine months before his death, Joseph was blessed by his father on his own death bed. At that time he told Joseph, "You shall live to lay out all the plan of all the work that God requires at your hand" (Proctor, Proctor, p.434). He did not promise Joseph a long life, but Joseph was overjoyed to learn that he would finish his work. He had obviously already accepted the prospect of his early death.

As his time drew nearer, Joseph was resigned to his impending death in an almost grateful way. At a special meeting of the Twelve in late March 1844, after placing keys and powers upon the assembled group, Joseph said, "the Lord is going to let me rest a while." He felt this was essential in order that his impending death would not cause keys to be lost. After this he said, even though he felt his death was near, "I feel that I am free" (Porter & Black, p.309).

Such resignation did not mean, however, that he would cooperate in his own execution. He knew a trip to Carthage would mean death. At a Nauvoo Municipal Court hearing on May 6, 1844, Joseph resisted going to a Carthage court to answer charges of slander by Francis M. Higbee. At that time in the Nauvoo Court, Joseph had given as a reason that he knew of "a conspiracy which has for some time been brewing against the life of your petitioner" (HC 6:358).

It was for this reason that early on the morning of June 23, 1844, Joseph decided to flee Nauvoo with his brother Hyrum, Willard Richards, and Porter Rockwell, believing that with him out of the city, his people would be safer. After the martyrdom, even Governor Ford thought that would have been the best solution.

Unfortunately, after crossing the river to flee west, Joseph was visited by a delegation his wife sent to urge him to return and give himself up to Carthage authorities. Joseph agreed but said, "If they had let me alone, there would have been no bloodshed, but Now I expect to be butchered" (*Wandle Mace Autobiography*, p.144). Yet in the back of his mind, Joseph must have been troubled by the possibility of an all-out war by the state upon Nauvoo as there had been by Missouri against the Far West Saints. And so, as Joseph returned to face his inevitable death, he was satisfied that if his sacrifice was not sufficient to save his people and beloved city, at least there could be no regrets. In his last speech to the Nauvoo Legion only a few days previously, he had declared, "I am ready to be offered a sacrifice for this people. . . You are a good people; therefore I love you with all my heart. Greater love hath no man than that he should lay down his life for his friends. You have stood by me in the hour of trouble, and I am willing to sacrifice my life for your preservation" (HC, 6:500). And so, with resignation and almost relief, Joseph turned back from safety and freedom for the sake of his people and his Church, as many Christian prophets had done before him.

Such a turn of events, however, had not taken Joseph unprepared for what he considered the inevitable. Before his surrender at Carthage, Joseph had given directions to his Council of Twelve about how he should be buried (Hill, p.5). This was his personal preparation for death but he was more concerned about his people. Had he prepared them properly?

Only eleven days before the jail attack, Joseph preached in the grove east of the Temple. In spite of a heavy rain, the people would not leave while the Prophet was speaking nor would he end the talk prematurely; he felt it might be the last opportunity to advise the people for whom he was to sacrifice his life. With the consciousness of his approaching death, he read to the people the third chapter of Revelation, which included these words: "Remember therefore, how thou hast received and heard, and hold fast and repent. . . behold I have set before thee an open door, and no man can shut it" (Rev. 3:3,8).

Joseph's fatalistic remarks to his many friends both before and during that final ride to Carthage are numerous and well-recorded: "I wish I could get Hyrum

125

out of the way, so that he may live to avenge my blood" (HC 6:20). To Daniel
Wells on the way to Carthage, he said, "I wish you to cherish my memory" (HC
6:554). "I am going like a lamb to the slaughter . . . it shall be said of me 'He was
murdered in cold blood!'" (HC 6:554-55).

The last direct narrative of the Prophet to his scribes before his death was
a prophesy on his approaching martyrdom. "I told Stephen Markham that if
Hyrum and I were ever taken again we would be massacred, or I was not a
prophet of God" (HC 6:546).

And finally, after Joseph was illegally incarcerated in the Carthage jail,
according to Nauvoo letter writer Sally Randall, he sent word to the Church in
Nauvoo "to read the 6(th) chapter of Revelation and take particular notice from
the 8(th) to the 12(th) verse" (Godfry, Godfry & Derr, p.142). The words found
in those verses were certainly prophetic and must surely have given the Saints
reason to suspect the possibility of the Prophet's coming martyrdom. Verse 8
reads, "And I looked, and behold a pale horse; and his name that sat on him was
Death," and verse nine reads, "And when he had opened the fifth seal, I saw
under the altar the souls of them that were slain for the word of God, and for the
testimony which they held" (Rev.6:8-9).

The summer after Joseph's death, Orson Hyde was quoted by Samuel
Richards in a letter: " From many things which he said and did, it is evident that
he knew an eventful period had arrived, that his exit was at hand, for he said, 'I
will die for this people' and he has gone" (Porter & Black, p.310).

B. H. Roberts, a lifelong scholar of Joseph Smith and Mormonism,
observed in connection with Joseph's King Follett Discourse that he

"lived his life in crescendo. From small beginnings, it rose in breadth and power as he neared its close. As a teacher he reached the climax of his career in this discourse. After it there was but one thing more he could do – seal his testimony with his blood. This he did less than three months later. Such is not the manner of life of false prophets." (Smith, p. 356 fn.)

It was painfully evident that Joseph, knowing his exit was at hand and that it was ordained of God, felt he should let the Lord direct him those final days and hours, regardless of what rational thought might suggest. Gilbert Belnap recorded in his autobiography that he remembered the Prophet saying, "Although I possessed the means of escape, yet I submit without a struggle and repair to the place of slaughter" (Andrus & Andrus, p.181). John Taylor, who was with him during that time, later reported, "I heard him state, in reply to an interrogatory, made either by myself or some one in my hearing, in relation to the best course to pursue; 'I am not now acting according to my best judgment,'" (HC 7:120). To face certain death and not act in one's own self-interest is certainly not the portrait of a pretender. To believe otherwise is comparable to insisting that the sun is not a source of light or that reason should not be a function of the human mind.

CONCLUSION

So – have the preceding pages proven that Joseph Smith was truly a prophet of God? Of course not – and that was not the author's intent. No writer sets out to "prove" that Moses or David or Abraham or Mohammed or Buddha were truly prophets or what their followers claim them to be. Such beliefs are based on study and prayer and faith. It is of some significance, however, that few writers ever set out to "disprove" the prophetic callings of such personages – except for the Prophet Joseph Smith. In his case there appears no end to the parade of religious "scholars" who are convinced he has deluded millions of people around the world and he must be "exposed."

Such a parade therefore leads to the logical question of why? Are the other religious prophets and founders ignored by the debunkers because evidence of their "callings" are so much more credible?

The answer, of course, is that if anything, the evidence is in most cases far less credible. Their immunity to charges of fraud is generally the result of community or family traditions, a remoteness in time, and a sizable following. The same obstacles held back the acceptance of those other faiths, including Christianity, in their infancy. There appears little doubt that as generations in the Church of Jesus Christ of Latter-day Saints are added to, as time passes and as conversions occur, prejudice and harassment will lessen. In the meantime, however, such bigotry is a reality and the only defense against it is knowledge.

The passage of time is an unchanging factor and a more sizable following will come only with the factor of time. Tradition, however, as other world religions have proven, can be changed. Knowledge is always an effective opponent of blind tradition and hopefully that is what this book has offered.

Tradition told the neighbors of Jesus's family that a prophet could not possibly come out of Nazareth, just as the traditions of nineteenth- and twentieth-century America have convinced so many religious traditionals that John Greenleaf Whittier, the poet, was mistaken when he said that "Once in the world's history we were to have a Yankee prophet, and we have had him in (Joseph) Smith" (Burton, p.20). Millions of Greenleaf's fellow Americans would agree, however, that traditions need not be an obstacle to facts. And the facts have given birth to the testimony of millions that a prophet of the Lord truly did come "out of Palmyra."

REFERENCES

Ahlstrom, Sydney. *A Religious History of the American People*. New Haven: Yale Univ. Press, 1972.

Augustine, Saint. *City of God*. New York: Doubleday Pub., 1958.

Andrus, Hyrum L. *Joseph Smith, the Man and the Seer*. Salt Lake City: Deseret Book Co., 1976.

Andrus, Hyrum L. and Helen Mae Andrus. *They Knew the Prophet*. Salt Lake City: Deseret Bk. Co., 1974.

Aston, Warren P. and Michaela Knoth. *In the Footsteps of Lehi*. Salt Lake City: Deseret Book Co., 1994.

Barrett, Ivan J. *Joseph Smith and the Restoration*. Provo, Utah: BYU Press, 1974.

Backman, Milton V., Jr. *Eyewitness Accounts of the Restoration*. .Salt Lake City: Deseret Book Co., 1983.

Backman, Milton V., Jr. *The Heavens Resound*. Salt Lake City: Deseret Book Co., 1983.

Backman, Milton V., Jr. and Richard O. Cowan, *Joseph Smith and the Doctrine and Covenants*. Salt Lake City: Deseret Book Co., 1992.

Berger, Max. *The British Traveller in America, 1836 - 1860*. New York: Columbia Univ. Press, 1943.

Black, Susan Easton and Tate, Charles D. Jr. (eds). *Joseph Smith: The Prophet, The Man*. Provo, Utah: Religious Studies Center, BYU, 1993.

Bloom, Harold. *The American Religion*. New York: Simon & Schuster, 1992.

Book of Mormon. Salt Lake City: The Church of Jesus Christ of Latter-day Saints, 1981.

Brown, Henry. *The History of Illinois, from its First Discovery and Settlement to the Present Time*. New York: Winchester Press, 1844.

Brough, R. Clayton and R. D. Griffin. *Scientific Support for Scripture Stories*.

Bountiful, Utah: Horizon Pub, 1992.

Burton, Alma P. (ed). *Discourses of the Prophet Joseph Smith.* Salt Lake City: Deseret Book Co., 1977.

Butler, John. *John Butler Autobiography* (typescript). Provo, Utah: Harold B. Lee Library, Special collections.

Cannon, Donald Q. and Lyndon W. Cook (eds). *Far West Record.* Salt Lake City: Deseret Book Co., 1983.

Cannon, George Q. *Life of Joseph Smith the Prophet.* Salt Lake City: Deseret Book Co., 1986.

Card, Orson Scott. *A Storyteller in Zion: Essays and speeches.* Salt Lake City: Bookcraft, 1993.

Cheeseman, Paul R. *Ancient Writing on Metal Plates.* Bountiful, Utah: Horizon Pub., 1985.

Church Educational System. *Church History in the Fulness of Times.* Salt Lake City: Church of Jesus Christ of Latter-day Saints, 1989.

Conkling, J. Christopher. *A Joseph Smith Chronology.* Salt Lake City: Deseret Book Co., 1979.

Cook, Lyndon W. *James Arlington Bennett and the Mormons.* BYU Studies, Vol. 19:2, pp. 247-49.

Crowther, Duane S. *The Prophecies of Joseph Smith.* Salt Lake City: Bookcraft, 1963.

Deseret News, *1991 - 1992 Church Almanac.* Salt Lake City: Deseret News, 1991.

DeTocqueville, Alexis. *Democracy in America* (2 vols.). New York: Random House, 1990.

Diringer, David. *The Hand Produced Book.* New York: 1953.

Doctrine and Covenants. Salt Lake City: Church of Jesus Christ of Latter-day Saints, 1981.

Ehat, Andrew F. and Lyndon W.Cook. *The Words of Joseph Smith..* Provo, Utah:

BYU Press, 1980.

Ferm, Vergilius (ed.). *Classics of Protestantism*. New York: Philosophical
Library, 1959.

Foote, Warren. *Autobiography of Warren Foote*. Springville, Utah: Garth
Killpack, 1984.

Ford, Thomas. *A History of Illinois* (2 vols.). Chicago: Lakeside Press, 1945.

Frost, John. *Indian Wars of the United States*. New York: Miller, Orton &
Mulligan, 1856.

Givens, George W. *In Old Nauvoo: Everyday Life in the City of Joseph*. Salt Lake
City: Deseret Book Co., 1990.

Godfrey, Kenneth W. and Audrey M. Godfrey and Jill Mulvay Derr. *Women's
Voices*. Salt Lake City: Deseret Book Co., 1982.

Griffith, Michael T. *Refuting the Critics*. Bountiful, Utah: Horizon Pub., 1993.

Hancock, Mosiah. *Mosiah Hancock Journal*. Provo, Utah: Harold B. Lee
Library, Special Collections.

Hatch, Nathan O. *The Democratization of American Christianity*. New Haven:
Yale Univ. Press, 1989.

Hill, Donna. *Joseph Smith, the First Mormon*. New York: Doubleday & Co.,
1977.

Hilton, Lynn M. and Hope Hilton. *In Search of Lehi's Trail*. Salt Lake City:
Deseret Book Co., 1976.

History of the Church of Jesus Christ of Latter-day Saints (7 vols.). Salt Lake
City: Deseret Book Co., 1980.

Jessee, Dean C. (ed.). *The Personal Writings of Joseph Smith*. Salt Lake City:
Deseret Book Co., 1984.

Johnson, Allen (ed.). *Dictionary of American Biography*. (Vol. 1) New York:
Scribner's, 1946.

Journal of Discourses. Liverpool: F. D. Richards (pub), 1855.

Kimball, Stanley B. *The Anthon Manuscript: People, Primary Sources and Problems.* Provo, Utah: BYU Studies, Spring 1970, pp 325-52.

Lamb, Martin T. *The Golden Bible; Or, The Book of Mormon. Is It From God?* New York: Pub., n.a., 1887.

Lambert, Neal E. (ed.). *Literature of Belief.* Provo, Utah: BYU Press, 1981.

Launius, Roger D. and John E. Hallwas (eds.). *Kingdom on the Mississippi. Revisited.* Urbana, Illinois: University of Ill. Press, 1996.

Loudon, Archibald. *A Selection of Some of the Most Interesting Narratives of Outrages Committed by the Indians in Their Wars With the White People. (reprint of 1808 edition)* New York: Arno Press, 1971.

Ludlow, Daniel H. *Encyclopedia of Mormonism (4 vols.).* New York: Macmillan Pub. Co., 1992.

Mace, Wandle. *Wandle Mace Autobiography (typescript).* Provo, Utah: Harold B. Lee Library, n.d.

Madsen, Truman. *Joseph Smith Among the Prophets (pamphlet).* Salt Lake City: Deseret Book Co., 1966.

Madsen, Truman. *Joseph Smith the Prophet.* Salt Lake City: Bookcraft, 1989.

Marryat, Captain Frederick. *Diary in America.* London: Nicholas Vane (pubs.), 1960.

Messenger & Advocate. Vol. 1, October 1834.

Miller, David E. and Della M. Miller. *Nauvoo: The City of Joseph.* Santa Barbara: Peregrine Smith, Inc., 1974.

Most Holy Principle, The (3 vols.). Murray, Utah: Gems Pub. Co., 1970.

Mulder, William and A. Russell Mortensen (eds.). *Among the Mormons.* Lincoln, Nebraska: University of Nebraska Press, 1973.

Newell, Linda King and Valeen Tippetts Avery. *Mormon Enigma:.Emma Hale Smith..* Garden City, New York: Doubleday & Co., 1984.

Nibley, Preston (ed.). *History of Joseph Smith by His Mother, Lucy Mack Smith.*

Salt Lake City: Bookcraft, 1958.

Noble, Joseph. *Joseph Noble Autobiography* (typescript). Provo, Utah: Harold B. Lee Library, Special Collections, n.d.

Mormons and Mormonism, by a non-Mormon. S.L.C., Utah: 1899.

O'Dea, Thomas F. *The Mormons.* Chicago: Univ. of Chicago Press, 1957.

Olsen, Steven L. *Cosmic Urban Symbolism in the Book of Mormon.* BYU Studies, Winter 1983, pp. 79-92.

Pearl of Great Price. Salt Lake City: The Church of Jesus Christ of Latter-day Saints, 1981.

Pidgen, Charles. *House of Shame.* New York: *Cosmopolitan,* 1912.

Porter, Larry C. and Susan Easton Black. *The Prophet Joseph; Essays on the Life and Mission of Joseph Smith..* Salt Lake City: Deseret Book Co., 1988.

Pratt, Parley P. *Autobiography of Parley P. Pratt.* Salt Lake City: Deseret Book Co., 1973.

Proctor, Scot Facer and Maurine Jensen Proctor (eds.). *The Revised and Enhanced History of Joseph Smith by His Mother.* Salt Lake City: Bookcraft, 1996.

Pulsipher, John. *John Pulsipher Autobiography* (typescript). Provo, Utah: Harold B. Lee Library, Special Collections.

Richards, Robert (pseud.). *The California Crusoe; or, the Lost Treasure Found, A Tale of Mormonism.* London: Parker Pub., 1854.

Roberts, B. H. *A Comprehensive History of the Church of Jesus Christ of Latter-day Saints.* (six vols.) Provo, Utah: BYU Press, 1965.

Shera, Jesse H. *Foundations of the Public Library.* Chicago: Univ. of Chicago Press, 1949.

Shipps, Jan and John W. Welch (eds.). *The Journals of William E. McLellin 1831-1836.* Provo, Utah and Urbana, Ill: BYU Studies and Univ. of Ill. Press, 1994.

Smith, Hyrum M. and Janne M. Sjodahl. *Doctrine and Covenants Commentary* Salt Lake City: Deseret Book Co., 1976.

Smith, Joseph. *History of the Church of Jesus Christ of Latter-day Saints* (8 vols.). Salt Lake City: Deseret Book Co., 1976.

Smith, Joseph Fielding (ed.). *Teachings of the Prophet Joseph Smith.* Salt Lake City: Deseret Book Co., 1977.

Smucker, Samuel M. *The Religious, Social, and Political History of the Mormons.* New York: Hurst & Co, 1881.

Sorenson, John L.and Melvin J. Thorne (eds.). *Rediscovering the Book of Mormon.* Salt Lake City and Provo: Deseret Book Co. and F.A.R.M.S., 1991.

Stark, Rodney. *The Rise of Christianity.* Princeton, N.J.: Princeton Univ. Press, 1996.

Times and Seasons, Nauvoo, Illinois, 1839 - 1846.

Vogel, Dan (ed.). *Early Mormon Documents, Vol. 1.* Salt Lake City: Signature Books, 1996.

Wallace, Arthur. *Can Mormonism Be Proved Experimentally?* Los Angeles, Cal.: Wallace (pub), 1973.

Washburn, J. Nile. *Book of Mormon Lands and Times.* Bountiful, Utah: Horizon Pub., 1974.

Welch, John W. *Chiasmus in the Book of Mormon.* Provo, Utah: F.A.R.M.S., 1994.

Welch, John W. (ed.). *Reexploring the Book of Mormon.* Salt Lake City: Deseret Book Co., 1991

Widtsoe, John A. *Joseph Smith: Seeker After Truth Prophet of God.* Salt Lake City: Bookcraft, 1993.